The Six Sigma Project Planner

The Six Sigma Project Planner

A Step-by-Step Guide to Leading a Six Sigma Project Through DMAIC

Thomas Pyzdek

McGraw-Hill

New York Chicago San Francisco Lisbon London
Madrid Mexico City Milan New Delhi San Juan
Seoul Singapore Sydney Toronto

Contents

Figures

Tables

Worksheets

Preface

My goals for *The Six Sigma Project Planner* are:

- Help the user identify worthy projects and move them steadily to successful completion.

- Help the user identify poorly conceived projects before devoting any time or resources to them.

- Help the user identify stalled projects and provide them with the attention they need to move forward again.

- Help the user decide when it's time to pull the plug on dead projects before they consume too much time and resources.

- Provide a record for the user that helps improve the project selection, management, and results tracking process.

Notice that I use the word "user," not "reader." The *Planner* isn't a textbook to be read; it is a working guide. Too often we read books or sit in classrooms and passively absorb the material. But a huge chasm exists between understanding the material intellectually and knowing how to use it to achieve results. Think of the *Planner* as a bridge over that chasm.

In the classroom the instructor says, "You must carefully evaluate a project proposal before deciding to pursue the project." Upon hearing this, your likely response would be to think, "Of course. That's obvious." However, you may not actually translate this thought into action when the proper time comes.

If you use the *Planner* properly, you'll be guided through a rigorous feasibility analysis (Figure 3, p. xvi) where you will assign a numerical rating to the project's sponsorship, benefits, timetable, resource availability, and much more. The proposed project will be assigned an overall score that can be used to compare it with other projects. You might choose to have the project evaluated by others on the team, providing a basis for discussion and consensus-building. In the end, you will make an informed decision. That decision may well be to pursue another project, thereby avoiding a false start and a waste of your time. If the decision is to go ahead with the project, it will be because the chances for success are excellent.

In other words, the *Planner* is about *getting results* rather than merely learning for the sake of knowledge acquisition. It's about *using* what you learned in your Black Belt or Green Belt training. The *Planner* provides brief overviews of some topics, but for the most part it is assumed that you have received training in the tools and techniques of Six Sigma. If you haven't, you'll need to attend classes or consult in-depth reference books, such as *The Six Sigma Handbook*.

Introduction

One day, several years ago, I received a call from a colleague who was organizing a conference on quality improvement in the healthcare industry. He asked if I could help him find a speaker who had successfully completed an improvement project involving healthcare processes. I had just begun consulting for an integrated healthcare organization that had been pursuing TQM for a number of months, so I called the Manager of Continuous Improvement and asked her. "No problem," she said. "We have over 50 projects in the works, and some have been underway for several months. I'm sure that we can find one to showcase at the conference."

She was wrong. Not a single project had produced tangible results. The organization had top-level commitment, the resources had been allocated and spent, people had been trained, teams were in place and empowered, but nothing had come from all of the effort. Research has shown that this situation is not uncommon with TQM deployments. Is it any wonder that TQM fell out of favor with the business community?

Six Sigma is different. It demands results. These results are delivered by projects that are tightly linked to customer demands and enterprise strategy. The *Six Sigma Project Planner* is designed to help the serious Six Sigma organization choose and complete projects that pay off. The *Planner* is designed specifically for use with Six Sigma projects. It integrates the project management body of knowledge as defined by the Project Management Institute and the Define-Measure-Analyze-Improve-Control (DMAIC) Six Sigma format for process improvement projects. It combines project management and business process improvement in a way that greatly improves the chances for success.

How to Use *The Six Sigma Project Planner*

The Six Sigma Project Planner is designed to implement the Project Planning and DMAIC phases of the process shown in Figure 1. It also addresses some issues encountered in the post-project phase. The assumption is that the enterprise has completed the project selection phase and that Six Sigma Green Belts and Black Belts are choosing their projects from a portfolio of project candidates approved by Senior Leadership.[1] The *Planner* is *not* a textbook on Six Sigma tools and techniques. It is assumed that the user of the *Planner* has been through the appropriate training class for his or her role in the project. For example, the project Black Belt will have received training as a Black Belt and knows what is meant when the *Planner* tells him or her to perform a gauge R&R study. For the trained individual, the *Planner* provides direction on when a particular Six Sigma tool or technique should be employed, assuming that the project team includes personnel who understand the tools. It also provides numerous worksheets and summary pages to implement the tools effectively.

---

[1] The process of developing a portfolio of projects driven by customers and enterprise strategy is treated in depth in Chapters 3 and 6 of *The Six Sigma Handbook*.

Figure 1. The Six Sigma Project Process Flow

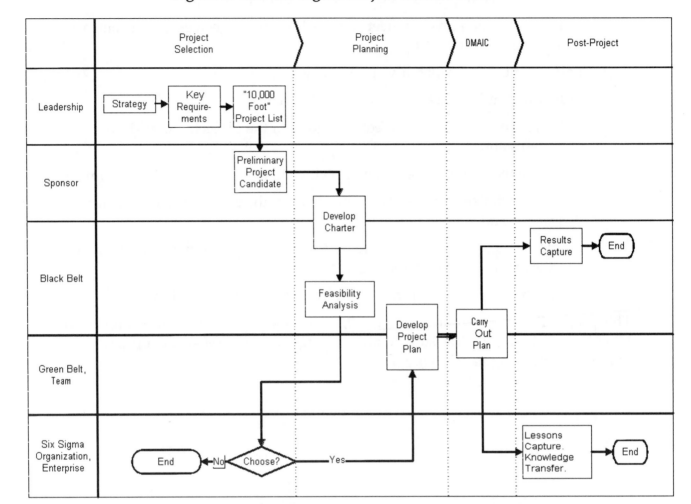

The *Planner* is designed to guide the project along a path that will lead to meeting the project's goals with minimum expenditure of effort and resources. There are several checkpoints built into the *Planner* where the project may be terminated successfully without completing the entire *Planner* or DMAIC cycle. The logical process flow is as follows:

1. Define the project's goals and deliverables.

   a. If these are not related to the organization's strategic goals and objectives, stop. The project is not a Six Sigma project. This does not necessarily mean that it isn't a "good" project or that the project shouldn't be done. There are many worthwhile and important projects that are not Six Sigma projects.

2. Define the current process.

3. Analyze the measurement systems.

4. Measure the current process and analyze the data using exploratory and descriptive statistical methods.

   a. If the current process meets the goals of the project, establish control systems and stop, else ...

5. Audit the current process and correct any deficiencies found.

   a. If the corrected process meets the goals of the project, establish control systems and stop, else …

6. Perform a process capability study using SPC.

   a. Identify and correct special causes of variation.

   b. If the controlled process meets the goals of the project, establish control systems and stop, else …

7. Optimize the current process by applying statistically designed experiments.

   a. If the optimized process meets the goals of the project, establish control systems and stop, else …

8. Employ breakthrough strategy to develop and implement an entirely new process that meets the project's goals.

9. Establish control and continuous improvement systems and stop.

This project flow is illustrated in Figure 2, which also shows the relationship between DMAIC and the Define-Measure-Analyze-Design-Verify (DMADV) approach used in Design for Six Sigma (DFSS).

Figure 2. Map of Six Sigma Project Flow[2]

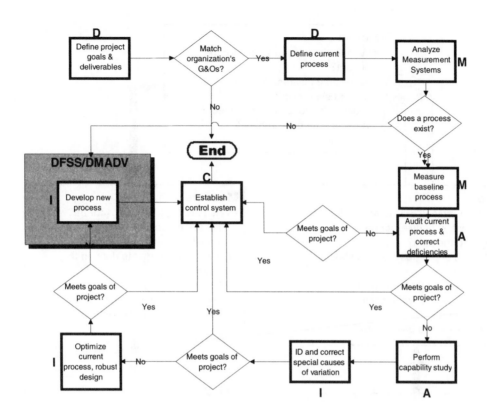

It will often happen that there are unresolved issues relating to one or more items in a particular worksheet. At the bottom of many worksheets you will find a box where you can assign a number for the issue. The Appendix provides an Issues List (p. 200) where you can describe issues in greater detail, as well as provide information on the issue resolution plan.

Some projects don't require all of the detail in the *Planner*. The documentation required for all projects is called the official project plan. Those sections of the *Planner* that are part of the official project plan are identified with a superscript asterisk (*) and a footnote. These materials, at a minimum, should be included for all projects.

The *Planner* is designed to provide complete documentation for any Six Sigma project. The worksheets in the *Planner* can be photocopied and placed in a three-ring binder after completion. The completed project document provides a ready reference for others pursuing similar projects. A library of such documents provides a wealth of information about how to conduct successful projects in the organization.

---

[2] Thanks to Michael Littleton of Boeing Satellite Systems for originally diagramming this process flow.

Figure 3. Six Sigma Project DMAIC Cycle Questions

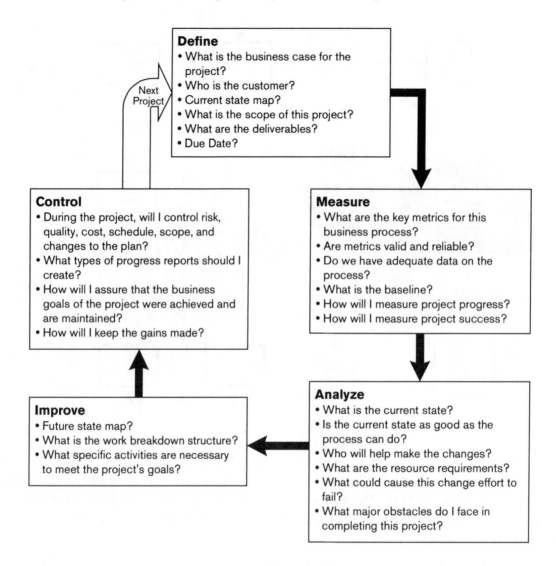

The Six Sigma Project Planner

Chapter 1
Planning

Develop the Project Charter

Project Charter*

Project charters (sometimes called *project scope statements*) should be prepared for each project and subproject. The project charter includes the project justification, the major deliverables, and the project objectives. It forms the basis of future project decisions, including the decision of when the project or subproject is complete. The project charter is used to communicate with stakeholders and to allow scope management as the project moves forward.

The Project Charter Document

The project charter is a written document issued by the project sponsor. The project charter gives the project team authority to use organizational resources for project activities. Use Worksheet 1 to document the charter for this project. Instructions for completing the Project Charter Statement follow the form.

---

* Part of the official project plan.

Worksheet 1. Project Charter Statement

Project Name/Number			
Sponsoring Organization			
Project Sponsor	Name:		Phone:
	Office Location:		Mail Stop:
Project Black Belt	Name:		Phone:
	Office Location:		Mail Stop:
Project Green Belt	Name:		Phone:
	Office Location:		Mail Stop:

Team Members (Name)	Title / Role	Phone	Office Location	Mail Stop

Principal Stakeholders	Title / Role	Phone	Office Location	Mail Stop

Date Chartered:	Project Start Date:	Target Completion Date:
Revision: N/C	Number: 0	Date:
	Sponsor Approval Signature:	

Project Name/Number:

Project Mission Statement

Problem Statement

Project Scope

Business Need Addressed by This Project

Product or Service Created by This Project (Deliverables)

Resources Authorized for This Project

Table 1. Instructions for Completing the Project Charter Statement Form

Field	Contents
Project Name/Number	Enter a short title for the project. If your organization has a project numbering system, include the assigned number.
Sponsoring Organization	Enter the name of the lowest-level organization that includes all processes changed by the project. This organizational unit must agree to sponsor the project.
Project Sponsor	The sponsor should be the process owner or line management at a level that can allocate resources for the project.
Project Black Belt	Enter the name and contact information of the Six Sigma Black Belt assigned to this project. If the project is being worked by a team of Black Belts, enter the name of the lead Black Belt responsible for the project.
Project Green Belt	Enter the name and contact information of the Green Belt project leader whose area is most directly impacted by the project.
Team Members	Enter the names and contact information of the core team members.
Principal Stakeholders	Enter the names and contact information of the people, other than the sponsor, who have a direct interest in the outcome of the project. E.g., customer, supplier, functional area manager, supervisor, responsible engineering authority, union leaders, etc.
Date Chartered	Enter the date that the charter was accepted and signed by the sponsor.
Project Start Date	Enter the date that the project is scheduled to begin. Update when the actual start date is known.
Target Completion Date	Enter the date when the project's deliverables are expected to be completed.
Revision	Charter revision tracking information.
Sponsor Approval Signature	Obtain the signature of the sponsor. Before signing, the sponsor should enter all project-related meetings into his or her schedule.

Project Name/Number	Since the charter is a two-page document, the project's ID information is repeated.
Project Mission Statement	State in clear and concise terms what this project will accomplish for the organization or its customers. Do not begin until every member of the project team and the sponsor are in agreement with the mission.
Problem Statement	Describe the "burning platform" for this project. Why is this project necessary?
Project Scope	Define the boundaries for this project. What will be addressed? What will not be addressed?
Business Need Addressed by This Project	Why should the problems described in the problem statement be solved? How will the business or its customers benefit from this project? How will this project improve quality, cycle time, costs, customer satisfaction, or competitiveness?
Product or Service Created by This Project (Deliverables)	Specifically, what will be created by this project? E.g., increased sales, reduced warranty expense, lower costs, shorter cycle time, etc.
Resources Authorized for This Project	List significant resources that must be made available and those that will be consumed to support this project. Examples: raw materials, machine time, overtime pay, operations personnel, etc.

Conduct a Feasibility Analysis

Is This a Valid Project?

Before launching a significant effort to solve a business problem, be sure that it is the correct problem and not just a symptom. Is the "defect" you are trying to eliminate something the customer cares about or even notices? Is the design requirement really essential, or can engineering relax the requirement? Is the performance metric really a key business driver, or is it arbitrary? Conduct a project validation analysis and describe your findings on the following page. Suggested techniques: interrelationship digraph, cause-and-effect diagram.

Figure 4. Example of Project Validation Analysis

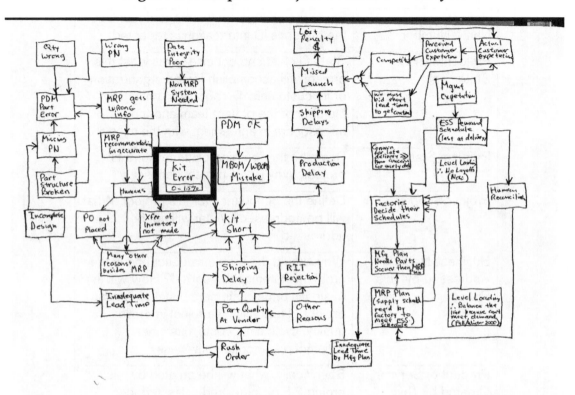

Note: In this real-life example, the originally proposed Six Sigma project is indicated in the box labeled "Kit Error," which is enclosed in a bold box in Figure 4. The true problem was that kits were arriving at the assembly process with parts missing,[1] shown in the box labeled "Kit Short." This project validation analysis indicated that kitting errors accounted for only a small percentage of the kits that arrived at the assembly process incomplete or incorrect. Several Six Sigma projects must be initiated to deal with the root causes of this problem.

---

[1] This would be the problem statement in the project charter. The business case for this project would be "Shipments are delayed because of incomplete assemblies."

Worksheet 2. Project Validation Analysis

Feasibility Analysis Summary

So, Mr. or Ms. Black Belt, you have a valid project, one that addresses the causes of an important effect. But should you pursue it? Before you begin actual project planning, you should take some time to assess the probability that the project will succeed. Assessing Six Sigma projects is an art as well as a science. It is also critical to the success of Six Sigma and to the individual Black Belt. Far too many Black Belts fail because they are not discriminating enough in selecting projects. If project selection is systematically sloppy, the entire Six Sigma effort can fail.

Feasibility analysis is a combination of quantitative and qualitative analysis. It is quantitative in that numerical ratings are used and an overall project score is calculated. It is qualitative and subjective to a degree, because it requires interpretation of the situation and estimating probabilities, costs, commitments, etc. However, the rigor that goes with completing the assessment process will help you make better judgments regarding projects.

The numbers (weights, scores, acceptable length of projects, dollar cutoffs, etc.) are based on my own personal judgments from my experience and discussions with consulting clients. While I believe that they are valid, you should feel free to assign your own values or those of your leadership. The scale for each criterion ranges from 0 to 9 and the weights sum to 1.00, so the highest possible weighted score for a project is 9. By dividing your scores by 9 and multiplying by 100, you can convert them into percentages. For example, a score of 9 would be 100% and a score of 7.2 would be 80%.

The Six Sigma department or process excellence organization can compile summary listings of project candidates from the individual project assessments. Sorting the list in descending order provides a Pareto-like guide to the final decision on which projects to pursue. Each Black Belt or Green Belt will probably have his or her own list, which can also be sorted and used as a guide.

Worksheet 2. Six Sigma Project Evaluation

Project Name:	Project Number:
Black Belt:	Master Black Belt:
Overall Project Weighted Score:	Date of Assessment:

Criterion	Score	Weight	Weighted Score[2]
1. Sponsorship		0.23	
2. Benefits (specify main beneficiary)	Overall Benefit Score		
☐ 2.1 External Customer:			
☐ 2.2 Shareholder:		0.19	
☐ 2.3 Employee or Internal Customer:			
☐ 2.4 Other (e.g., supplier, environment):			
3. Availability of resources other than team		0.16	
4. Scope in terms of Black Belt effort		0.12	
5. Deliverable		0.09	
6. Time to complete		0.09	
7. Team		0.07	
8. Project charter		0.03	
9. Value of Six Sigma approach		0.02	
TOTAL (sum of weighted score column)		1.00	

Note: Any criterion scores of zero must be addressed before project is approved.

---

[2] Weighted score = project's score for each criterion times the weight for that criterion.

Sponsorship

Score	Interpretation
9	Director-level sponsor identified, duties specified, and sufficient time committed and scheduled in advance
3	Director-level sponsor identified, duties specified, and sufficient time committed but not scheduled
1	Willing director-level sponsor who has accepted charter statement
0	Director-level sponsor not identified or sponsor has not accepted the charter

2.0 Stakeholder Benefits[3]

"Tangible and verifiable benefits for a major stakeholder"

2.1 Stakeholder: External Customer

2.1.1 Customer Satisfaction

Score	Interpretation
9	Substantial and statistically significant increase in *overall* customer satisfaction or loyalty
3	Substantial and statistically significant increase in a *major subcategory* of customer satisfaction
1	Substantial and statistically significant increase in a *focused area* of customer satisfaction
0	Unclear or no customer satisfaction impact

---

[3] Several stakeholder benefit categories are shown in section 2. At least one stakeholder benefit category is required. Show benefit scores for each category. Then use your judgment to determine an overall benefit score for the project.

2.1.2 Quality Improvement (CTQ[4])

Score	Interpretation
9	10x or greater improvement in CTQ metric
5	5x to 10x improvement in CTQ metric
3	2x to 5x improvement in CTQ metric
1	Statistically significant improvement in CTQ metric, but less than 2x magnitude
0	Project's impact on CTQ metrics undefined or unclear

2.2 Stakeholder: Shareholder

2.2.1 Financial Benefits

Score	Interpretation
9	Hard net savings (budget or bid model change) greater than $500K. Excellent ROI.[5]
5	Hard net savings between $150K and $500K. Excellent ROI.
3	Hard net savings between $50K and $150K or cost avoidance greater than $500K. Good ROI.
1	Hard savings of at least $50K or cost avoidance between $150K and $500K. Acceptable ROI.
0	Project claims a financial benefit but has hard savings less than $50K, cost avoidance less than $150K, or unclear financial benefit.

2.2.2 Cycle Time Reduction

Score	Interpretation
9	Cycle time reduction that improves revenue, bid model, or budget by more than $500K. Excellent ROI.
5	Cycle time reduction that improves revenue, bid model, or budget by $150K to $500K. Excellent ROI.
3	Cycle time reduction that improves revenue, bid model, or budget by $50K to $150K or creates a cost avoidance of more than $500K. Good ROI.
1	Cycle time reduction that results in cost avoidance between $150K and $500K. Acceptable ROI.

---

[4] Critical to quality.

[5] Return on investment.

0	Project claims a cycle time improvement but has hard savings less than $50K, cost avoidance less than $150K, or unclear financial benefit from the improvement in cycle time.

2.2.3 Revenue Enhancement

Score	Interpretation
9	Significant increase in revenues, excellent ROI.
3	Moderate increase in revenues, good ROI.
1	Measurable increase in revenues, acceptable ROI.
0	Unclear or no revenue impact.

2.3 Stakeholder: Employee or Internal Customer

2.3.1 Employee Satisfaction

Score	Interpretation
9	Substantial and statistically significant increase in *overall* employee satisfaction.
3	Substantial and statistically significant increase in *a major element* of employee satisfaction.
1	Substantial and statistically significant increase in *a focused area* of employee satisfaction.
0	Unclear or no employee satisfaction impact.

2.4 Stakeholder: Other

2.4.1 Specify Stakeholder: _____

Benefits

Score	Interpretation
9	
5	

Score	Interpretation
3	
1	
0	Unclear or no benefit

3.0 Availability of Resources Other than Team

Score	Interpretation
9	Needed resources available when needed.
3	Limited or low priority access to needed resources.
1	Questionable resource availability.
0	Resources not available or excessive restrictions on access to resources.

4.0 Scope in Terms of Black Belt Effort

Score	Interpretation
9	Projected return substantially exceeds required return.
3	Projected return exceeds required return.
1	Projected return approximately equals required return.
0	Projected return not commensurate with required return.

Required return can be calculated as follows:[6]

(1) Length of project (months) = _____

(2) Proportion of Black Belt's time required (between 0 and 1) = _____

(3) Probability of success (between 0 and 1) = _____

---

[6] Thanks to Tony Lin of Boeing Satellite Systems for this heuristic.

Required[7] return = $83,333 x (1) x (2) ÷ (3) = $_____

Projected return: $_____

5.0 Deliverable

Score	Interpretation
9	New or improved process or product or service to be created is clearly and completely defined.
3	New or improved process or product or service to be created is defined.
0	Deliverable is poorly or incorrectly defined—for example, a deliverable that is really a tool, such as a process map.

6.0 Time to Complete

Score	Interpretation
9	Results realized in less than three months.
3	Results realized in three to six months.
1	Results realized in seven to 12 months.
0	Results will take more than 12 months to be realized.

7.0 Team Membership

Score	Interpretation
9	Correct team members recruited and time commitments scheduled.
3	Correct team members recruited, time committed but not scheduled.
1	Correct team members recruited.
0	Team members not recruited or not available.

---

[7] Based on expected Black Belt results of $1MM/year.

8.0 Project Charter

Score	Interpretation
9	All elements of the project charter are complete and acceptable. Linkage between project and deliverable is clear.
3	Project charter acceptable with minor modifications.
0	Project charter requires major revisions.

9.0 Value of Six Sigma Approach (DMAIC or Equivalent)

Score	Interpretation
9	Six Sigma approach essential to the success of the project. Black Belt/Green Belt skill set required for success.
3	Six Sigma approach helpful but not essential. Black Belt/Green Belt skill set can be applied.
0	Usefulness of Six Sigma approach not apparent. Specific Black Belt or Green Belt skills are not necessary.

The Project Plan

Project Metrics

At this point you know who the project's customers are and what they expect in the way of project deliverables. Now you must determine precisely how you will measure progress toward achieving the project's goals.

What Is the Total Budget for This Project?

Projects consume resources. To accurately measure project success, it is necessary to keep track of how these resources are used. The total project budget sets an upper limit on the resources this project will be allowed to consume. Knowing this value, at least approximately, is vital for resource planning.

Worksheet 5. Project Budget Development

Budget Item	Estimated Expenditure Range	Charge Account #	Authorization
Team Meetings			
Team Member Time			
Contract Work			
Materials			

How Will I Measure Project Success?

You should have one or more metrics for each project deliverable.

- Metrics should be selected to keep the project focused on its goals and objectives.

- Metrics should detect project slippage soon enough to allow corrective action to avert damage.

- Metrics should be based on customer or sponsor requirements.

Worksheet 6. Deliverables Metrics

Deliverable	Validation Metrics	Frequency of Measurement

Refining the Dollar Opportunity Estimates

Preliminary estimates of benefits were made previously during the initial planning. However, the data obtained by the team will allow the initial estimates to be made more precisely at this time.

Whenever possible, "characteristics" should be expressed in the language of management: dollars. One needn't strive for to-the-penny accuracy; a rough figure is usually sufficient. It is recommended that the finance and accounting department develop dollar estimates; however, in any case it is important that the estimates at least be accepted (in writing) by the accounting and finance department as reasonable. This number can be used to compute a return on investment (ROI) for the project.

As a general rule, dollar estimates are made conservatively. That is, they do not consider the dollar value of intangibles such as improved employee morale or customer satisfaction. The approach is usually to consider the cost of the current process and to compare it with the cost of operating the improved process. A recommended approach is to calculate the cost of a single error or problem, estimate the total number of errors or problems, and multiply to arrive at the dollar size of the opportunity. This is compared with the project's cost and time to determine the ROI.

Example #1: Cost of Incomplete or Inaccurate Customer Data

The Six Sigma project involved improving the quality of data in a customer database at a call center. Whenever a customer phones in, the representative looks for the customer's record in the database and verifies the information it contains. Based on a sample, it is estimated that about 11% of the records in the database are incorrect and require attention by the representative. Considering only direct costs (labor), the estimated opportunity is calculated as follows:

Figure 5. Example of Cost-Benefit Opportunity Calculations

Number of calls/year	1,300,000.
Average time to correct database	30 seconds (0.5 minutes)
Cost per minute	$1.75.
Size of opportunity	$1.75 x 0.5 x 1,300,000 x 0.11 = $125,125.
Estimated cost of project	$25,000. No additional operating expense is expected.
Estimated improvement	Reduce errors by 90%, to 1.1% incorrect records.
Savings	$125,125.00 – $12,512.50 = $112,612.50.
Time to complete	4 months.
First-year ROI	3 x ($112,612.50 / $25,000) x 100 = 1351%.

Worksheet 7. Dollar Opportunity Estimate

Error or Problem	Cost Now	Cost After Improvement	Savings	Accounting Concurrence
TOTAL				
Project ROI				
Accounting Concurrence				

How Will I Monitor Satisfaction with Project Progress?

Six Sigma projects have a significant impact on people while they are being conducted. It is important that the perspectives of all interested parties be periodically monitored to ensure that the project is meeting their expectations and not becoming too disruptive. The Black Belt should develop a means for obtaining this information, analyzing it, and taking action when the results indicate a need. Data collection should be formal and documented. Relying on "gut feeling" is not enough.

Means of monitoring[8]:

- Personal interviews
- Focus groups
- Surveys
- Meetings
- Comment cards
- Other:

---

[8] *Six Sigma Handbook,* Chapter 3.

Worksheet 8. Project Progress Satisfaction Metrics

Stakeholder Group	Metric	Means of Monitoring	Frequency	Responsibility
Customers				
Sponsors				
Process area personnel				
Team members				
Team member supervisors				

Identify Human Resources Needed to Complete the Project*

We can now identify our basic strategy for achieving the project goals, as summarized in Table 2.

Table 2. Strategies for Meeting the Project Goals

Situation	Action Indicated	Project Strategy
The process can meet the project goals if it is operated properly.	No additional action is necessary, other than ensuring that the process is properly maintained and operated according to established procedures.	*Discipline Strategy:* Establish systems to ensure proper maintenance, documentation, employee training, process monitoring, and process control.
The process can meet the project goals, but it is not doing so due to special causes of variation.	Identify and eliminate special causes of variation in the process.	*Control Strategy:* Provide SPC training to operating personnel, establish action plans to respond to out-of-control indications, develop improvement plans to identify and eliminate special causes of variation.
The process can meet the project goals if we implement the changes needed to optimize its performance.	Operate the process at the settings indicated by DOE findings.	*Optimization Strategy:* Prepare plans to implement optimal system and process settings as determined by the DOE.
Even if it were operated at optimum, the process cannot meet the project goals. Breakthrough to unprecedented performance levels is required to meet the project goals.	New process design is required.	*Breakthrough Strategy:* Develop entirely new systems designed to meet the project goals. Utilize the results of the benchmarking activity.

With the appropriate strategy determined, it is time to re-evaluate project team membership. Review Worksheet 1 (p. 2) to determine if the team as currently composed includes the knowledge, skills, abilities, and personal attributes (KSAP) needed to successfully implement the project strategy.

---

* Part of the official project plan.

24

Guidelines for Evaluating Team Member Candidates

- Do they possess a needed KSAP or certification?

- Are they willing to work on this project?

- Do they have sufficient time to work on this project?

    - Obtain resource calendars for planning and scheduling purposes

- Will their supervisor allow their involvement?

- What is their role?

    - Sponsor, team member, advisor, process operator, process supplier, customer, interested third party

Worksheet 9. Human Resources Assessment

		KSAPs	Willingness	Availability	Allowed?	
Candidates' Roles in the Project	Core Members					
	Sponsor(s)					
	Team Advisors					
	Process Operators					
	Process Suppliers					
	Project Customers					
	Other Role (specify)					

Identify Other Resources Needed to Complete the Project*

Examples of things to consider:

- Resource calendars for planning and scheduling
- Machinery needed
- Process time
- Materials
- Tool and die work
- Engineering prototypes
- Laboratory tests
- Gauges
- Measurement equipment
- Floor space, office space, and other facility requirements
- Furniture
- Plumbing, electrical wiring, etc.
- Ventilation and other environmental requirements
- Special storage requirements
- Clean rooms
- Safety equipment
- Forklifts, trucks, and other transportation
- Enterprise or legacy data access
- Special computer requirements (e.g., workstations, mainframes)
- Special software requirements (e.g., simulation software, CAD)
- Where will the resources come from?
- Whose permission do I need to obtain these resources?
- Special requirements (e.g., certification, safety issues)

---

* Part of the official project plan.

Worksheet 10. Project Resource Planning

Required Resource	Resource Owner	Availability	Issue #

Work Breakdown Structures (WBS)

The creation of work breakdown structures involves a process for defining the final and intermediate products of a project and their interrelationships. Defining project activities is complex. It is accomplished by performing a series of decompositions, followed by a series of aggregations. For example, a software project to develop an SPC software application would disaggregate the customer requirements into very specific engineering requirements. The customer requirement that the product create x-bar charts would be decomposed into engineering requirements such as subroutines for computing subgroup means and ranges, plotting data points, drawing lines, etc. Reaggregation would involve, for example, linking the various modules to produce an x-bar chart and display it on the screen.

Creating the WBS

The project deliverables expected by the project's sponsors were initially defined in the project charter (p. 2). Deliverables metrics are given in Worksheet 6, Deliverables Metrics (p. 19). For most Six Sigma projects, major project deliverables are so complex as to be unmanageable. Unless they are broken into components, it isn't possible to obtain accurate cost and duration estimates for each deliverable. WBS creation is the process of identifying manageable components or subproducts for each major deliverable. The process is pictured in Figure 6.

Figure 6. WBS Creation Process Flowchart

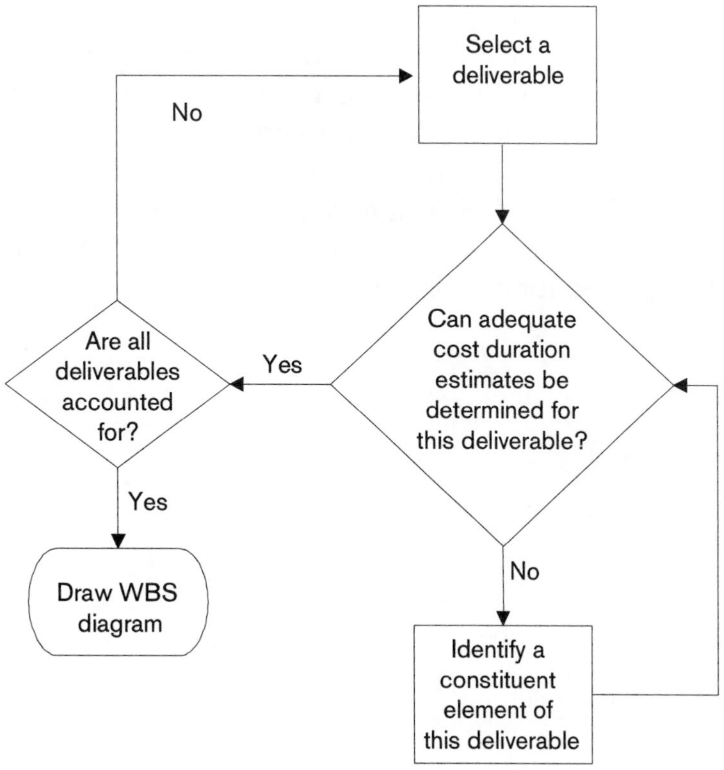

Figure 7. Example of a WBS

Wave Solder Improvement Project

```
                    ┌─────────────────────┐
                    │  Reduce Solder DPMO │
                    │    from 5000 to 50  │
                    └──────────┬──────────┘
        ┌──────────────────────┼──────────────────────┐
┌───────────────┐  ┌───────────────────────┐  ┌──────────────┐
│ Maintenance Plan│  │ Reduce top 3 defect types│  │ Establish SPC │
└───────────────┘  └───────────┬───────────┘  └──────────────┘
              ┌────────────────┼────────────────┐
      ┌──────────────┐  ┌──────────────────┐  ┌───────────┐
      │ Cold solder  │  │ No solder in hole│  │ Pad Lifts │
      └──────────────┘  └────────┬─────────┘  └───────────┘
                   ┌─────────────┴─────────────┐
           ┌──────────────┐            ┌─────────────────┐
           │ Simple Boards│            │ Complex Boards  │
           └──────────────┘            └────────┬────────┘
                              ┌─────────────────┴─────────────────┐
                      ┌────────────────┐                  ┌──────────────────┐
                      │ With heat sinks│                  │ Without heat sinks│
                      └───────┬────────┘                  └─────────┬────────┘
                     ┌────────┴────────┐                  ┌─────────┴────────┐
                 ┌──────────┐ ┌──────────┐          ┌──────────┐ ┌──────────┐
                 │ Product A│ │ Product B│          │ Product A│ │ Product B│
                 └──────────┘ └──────────┘          └──────────┘ └──────────┘
```

Complex Product B boards without heat sinks that have holes with no solder will be a subproject.

For simplicity, not all branches of the WBS are shown in Figure 7. The only branch fully developed is that of complex boards for the problem labeled "no solder in hole." On real projects, upper-level WBS often connect to "off-page connectors," which are circles with a letter or number reference to a lower-level WBS chart. The WBS process continues down to the level where the team feels it can clearly budget, schedule, and assign activities. Problems defined to this level are sometimes referred to as "tiny." The basic idea is to divide and conquer larger issues by reducing them to simple mini-projects. In this example, the WBS was terminated when a particular type of solder problem could be assigned to a team that includes a design engineer and a process engineer.

You may have noticed a resemblance between the WBS diagram and an organization chart. In fact, the idea behind the WBS is the same as the idea behind a formal organization: division of work. The work performed by an organization is generally too complex to be done by a single functional unit, so it is divided according to a logical scheme. The same is true for the WBS. You may wish to take advantage of this basic similarity to create the WBS. For example, Microsoft Word includes an organizational chart tool that can be adapted for creating the WBS diagram.

Worksheet 11. Project Work Breakdown Structure

Integration and Test[*]

Unless careful planning is done, the whole may be considerably less than the sum of its parts! Although the WBS makes it possible to tackle one big project by treating it as a collection of small subprojects, it does so by a process known as *disintegration*. At some point the subprojects (or subproducts or subprocesses) must be reintegrated and the whole system tested as a unit.

Inputs

The basis of the integration and test plan is the Integration Plan, the list of project deliverables (see Worksheet 6. Deliverable Metrics, p. 19), and the WBS. Together, these documents tell you what the project deliverables are, how they were decomposed, and how the project's sponsor will judge the project's success.

Integration Plan

"How will the complete system be tested and validated?"

Project Schedule Development[11]

Project Deadline

- What is the latest completion date that allows the project to meet its objective?

Project Deadline (get from project charter, p. 2)	

- What are the penalties for missing this date? Things to consider are lost market share, contract penalties, fines, lost revenues, etc.

---

[*] Part of the official project plan.

[11] For an alternative method of scheduling projects, see "Critical Chain Project Portfolio Management," pp. 191-193.

Worksheet 12. List of Penalties for Missing Deadline

Worksheet 13. Major Milestones and Target Dates

Milestone	Target Date

Project schedules are developed to ensure that all activities are completed, reintegrated, and tested on or before the project due date. A number of tools and techniques that help create, analyze, and manage project schedules will be discussed next. Software can be used to automate the calculations involved and to make it easier to identify scheduling conflicts and resource shortages. The output of the scheduling activity is a time chart (schedule) showing the start and finish times for each activity as well as its relationship to other activities in the project and responsibility for completing the activity. The schedule must identify activities that are critical in the sense that they *must* be completed on time to keep the project on schedule.

Don't accept the initial project schedule as a given. The information obtained in *preparing* the schedule can be used to *improve* it. Activities that the analysis indicates to be critical are prime candidates for improvement. Pareto analysis[12] can be used to identify those critical elements that are most likely to lead to significant improvement in overall project completion time. Cost data can be used to supplement the time data and the combined time/cost information can be analyzed using Pareto analysis. Always keep in mind that the project's deadline is a worst acceptable date, not the most desirable.

Activity Definition

Once the WBS is complete, it can be used to prepare a list of the activities (tasks) necessary to complete the project. Activities don't simply complete themselves. The resources, time, and personnel necessary to complete the activities must be determined. We now have the information we need to complete this portion of the project plan.

Activity Definition Inputs

To complete this portion of the project planner, you will need to refer to the WBS (p. 31) and the project charter (p. 2). Additional research will also be required to determine if similar projects or subprojects were conducted previously and, if so, what historical information for activity definitions, activity durations, and problems encountered should be reviewed. Document the findings using Worksheet 14. Historical Research Summary. If available, activity lists from similar projects should be obtained to use as templates. These can be placed into the *Planner* as supporting detail.

---

[12] *Six Sigma Handbook*, Chapter 8.

Worksheet 14. Historical Research Summary

Similar Project	Key Lessons	Issue #

Constraints—factors that limit the team's options—also need to be identified. Use Worksheet 15 to list the constraints and the plans for dealing with them.

Worksheet 15. Constraint Analysis

Constraint	Effect of Constraint	Planned Response to Constraint	Issue #

A common problem to guard against is *scope creep*. As activities are developed, be certain that they do not go beyond the project's original scope. Equally common is the problem of *scope drift*. In these cases, the project focus gradually moves away from its original charter. Since the activities are the project, this is a good place to carefully review the scope statement in the project charter (p. 2) to ensure that the project remains focused on its goals and objectives.

Activity Dependencies

Some project activities depend on others: sometimes a given activity may not begin until another activity is complete. For example, if the project involves building a house, the construction of the floor cannot begin until the foundation has been poured and had time to cure properly. Other activities can be done in parallel, simultaneously. The outside of the house can be painted while the drywall is being installed inside or while the roof shingles are being installed. The project plan and schedule must take these *dependencies* into account.

To sequence activities so they happen at the right time, you must link dependent activities and specify the type of dependency. The linkage is determined by the nature of the dependency. Activities are linked by defining the dependency between their finish and start dates, as shown below.

Figure 8. Types of Activity Dependencies

Activity Dependency Type	Example	Description
finish-to-start (FS)		Activity B cannot start until activity A finishes.
start-to-start (SS)		Activity B cannot start until activity A starts.
finish-to-finish (FF)		Activity B cannot finish until activity A finishes.
start-to-finish (SF)		Activity B cannot finish until activity A starts.

Worksheet 16. Activity Dependencies

Activity	Dependent On	Dependency Type	Responsible	Resources

Estimating Activity Duration

In addition to knowing the dependencies, to schedule the project you also need estimates of how long each activity might take. This information will be used by senior management to schedule projects for the enterprise and by the project manager to assign resources, to determine when intervention is required, and for various other purposes.

Duration Estimation Guidelines

It is seldom possible to know the activity duration exactly. A given activity duration estimate can be considered to be associated with a statistical probability of actually achieving it. In most traditional projects, the activity duration is provided by the person to whom the activity is assigned; this person usually includes a buffer that can be used if there are unforeseen, but probable problems. In scheduling and managing projects, it is helpful to know the magnitude of this buffer. Thus, in estimating the duration of activities for Six Sigma projects, we ask for not one but three estimates: optimistic, most likely, and pessimistic. These estimates are defined as follows:

Optimistic duration: the activity duration if the work proceeded exactly according to plan, with no delays or interruptions.

Most likely duration: the activity duration if we assume a typical pattern of delays and interruptions.

Pessimistic duration: the activity duration if we assume an unusually large number of delays and interruptions.

In general, duration estimates should be obtained from the person assigned responsibility for the activity. However, if this person is not on the project team, he or she should be made aware of the findings from the research conducted by the team. This would include research into the duration of similar activities on similar projects.

Note: In traditional project management, people are asked for deadlines or due dates for their tasks. They are then held accountable for meeting these due dates and punished if they fail to meet them. Under these circumstances, people will always provide pessimistic duration estimates. (Wouldn't you?) In Six Sigma environments, we develop and manage project schedules based on most-likely estimates or weighted average estimates (explained below). This means that there's a good chance of not meeting the projected task duration. Thus, although the project schedule must be managed, failure to meet a task duration target must be tolerated. Statistically, the project due date will be met if the *average* task duration is relatively close to that predicted.

Worksheet 17. Activity Duration Estimates

WBS Activity Description	Person Estimating Duration	Activity Duration Estimates			Weighted Average[13]	Issue #
		(a) Optimistic	(b) Most Likely	(c) Pessimistic		

---

[13] Weighted average = (a + 4b + c) / 6.

Gantt Charts

A Gantt chart shows the relationships among the project tasks, along with time estimates. The horizontal axis of a Gantt chart shows units of time (days, weeks, months, etc.). The vertical axis shows the activities to be completed. Bars show the estimated start time and duration of the various activities. Figure 9 illustrates a simple Gantt chart that can be created by hand. There are many types of Gantt charts, limited only by the needs of the project. The Gantt chart should show activity dependencies.

Figure 9. Gantt Chart of Schedule

Activity	Week 1	Week 2	Week 3	Week 4
1	███			
2		███	███	
3	███			
4			███	
5			███	
6				███

Milestone Charts

Gantt charts are often modified in various ways to provide additional information. One common variation is shown below. The *milestone* symbol (♦) represents an event (a point in time) rather than an activity (an interval of time). Unlike activities, milestones do not consume time or resources. When Gantt charts are modified in this way, they are sometimes called *milestone charts*. In the milestone chart below, uncompleted activity durations are shown as unfilled boxes. As activities are completed, the boxes are filled in.

Figure 10. Gantt/Milestone Chart of Actual vs. Scheduled Performance

Activity	Week 1	Week 2	Week 3	Week 4
1 (100%)	███			Today
2 (50%)		███		
3 (50%)	██			
4 (milestone)			♦	
5 (not started)				
6 (not started)				
7 (not started)				

Gantt charts and milestone charts can be modified to show additional information, such as who is responsible for a task, why a task is behind schedule, remedial action planned or already taken, etc. They are excellent tools for presenting a great deal of information in an easy-to-understand format.

Computer-Generated Gantt Charts

If the project team has access to project management software, it can use the software to draw Gantt and milestone charts. The chart below was created using Microsoft Project 2000. The chart indicates dependencies with arrows. However, pretty charts, attractive as they may be, are not a prerequisite for project success. Important, complex projects were planned and executed long before computers arrived!

Figure 11. Example of Computer Gantt/Milestone Chart

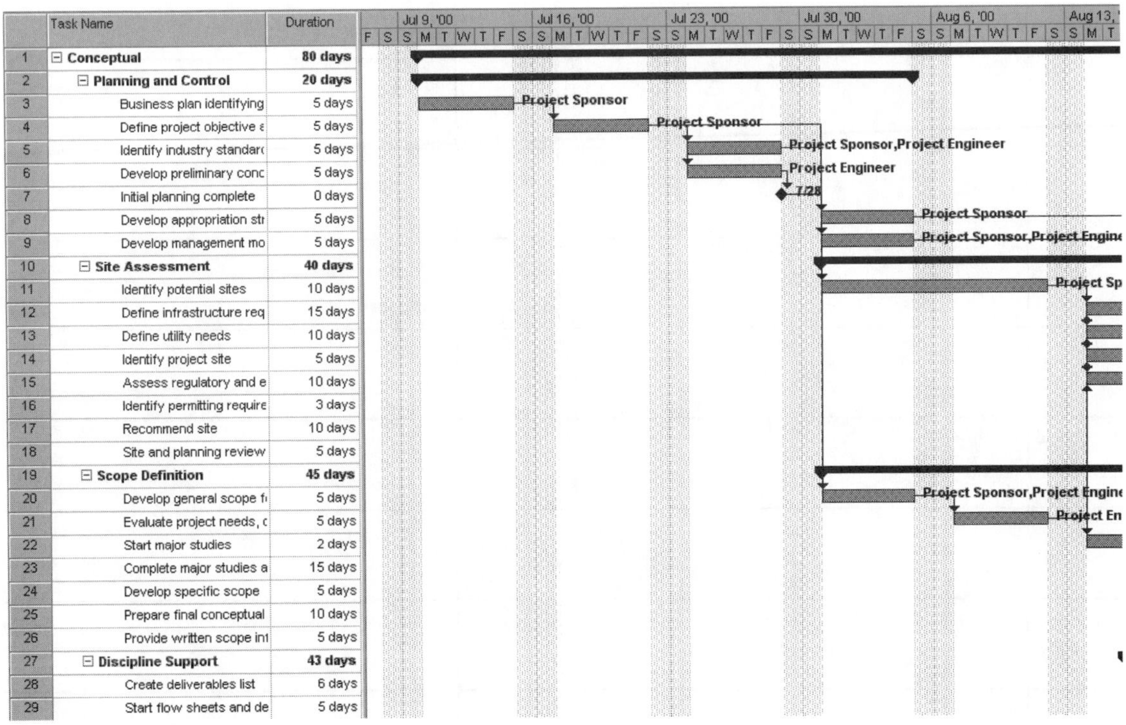

Worksheet 18. List of Activities

No.	Activity	No.	Activity

Worksheet 19. Project Gantt/Milestone Chart Template[14]

Project Name		Chart Creator		Date Created	
Period Covered		Comment			

Activity #	Time Period												
	1	2	3	4	5	6	7	8	9	10	11	12	13
1													
2													
3													
4													
5													
6													
7													
8													
9													
10													
11													
12													
13													
14													
15													
16													
17													
18													
19													
20													

---

[14] Spreadsheets and word processors can also be used to create these charts.

Worksheet 20. Project Gantt/Milestone Chart (Freehand Drawing Format)

Project Name		Chart Creator		Date Created	
Period Covered		Comment			

Network Diagrams

A project network diagram shows both the project logic and the project's critical path activities, i.e., those activities that, if not completed on schedule, will cause the project to miss its due date.

PERT- and CPM-Type Project Management Systems

Although useful, Gantt charts and their derivatives provide limited project schedule analysis capabilities. The successful management of large-scale projects requires more rigorous planning, scheduling, and coordinating of numerous, interrelated activities. To aid in these tasks, formal procedures based on the use of networks and network techniques were developed beginning in the late 1950s.

The most prominent of these procedures have been PERT (Program Evaluation and Review Technique) and CPM (Critical Path Method). The two approaches are usually referred to as PERT-type project management systems. The most important difference between PERT and CPM is that originally the time estimates for the activities were assumed to be deterministic in CPM and were probabilistic in PERT. Today, PERT and CPM actually constitute one technique and the differences are mainly historical. Modern project management tends more toward CPM than PERT.

CPM systems are used to:
- aid in planning and controlling projects
- determine the feasibility of meeting specified deadlines
- identify the most likely bottlenecks in a project
- evaluate the effects of changes in the project requirements or schedule
- evaluate the effects of deviating from schedule
- evaluate the effect of diverting resources from the project or redirecting additional resources to the project.

Project scheduling by CPM consists of four basic phases: planning, scheduling, improvement, and controlling.

The planning phase involves breaking the project into distinct activities. The time estimates for these activities are then determined and a network (or arrow) diagram is constructed, with each activity being represented by an arrow.

The ultimate objective of the scheduling phase is to construct a time chart showing the start and finish times for each activity as well as its relationship to other activities in the project. The schedule must identify activities that are critical in the sense that they *must* be completed on time to keep the project on schedule.

It is vital not to merely accept the schedule as a given. The information obtained in preparing the schedule can be used to improve it. Activities that the analysis indicates to be critical are candidates for improvement. Pareto analysis can be used to identify those critical elements that are most likely to lead to significant improvement in overall project completion time. Cost data can be used to supplement the time data. The combined time/cost information can be analyzed using Pareto analysis.

The final phase in CPM project management is project control. This includes the use of the network diagram and time chart for making periodic progress assessments. CPM network diagrams can be created by a computer program or constructed manually. (For details, see Appendix, p. 199.)

Figure 12. Example of Network Diagram

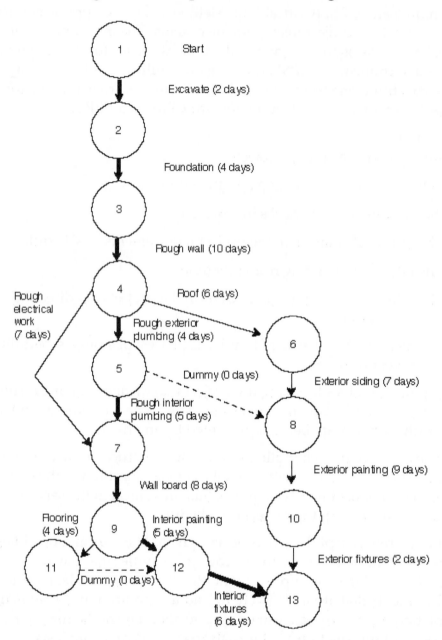

The bold line shows the critical path for this project. Figure 13 is a CPM network diagram from a popular software package. Red lines (thicker) indicate critical path activities and milestones.

Figure 13. Example of a Computer-Generated Network Diagram

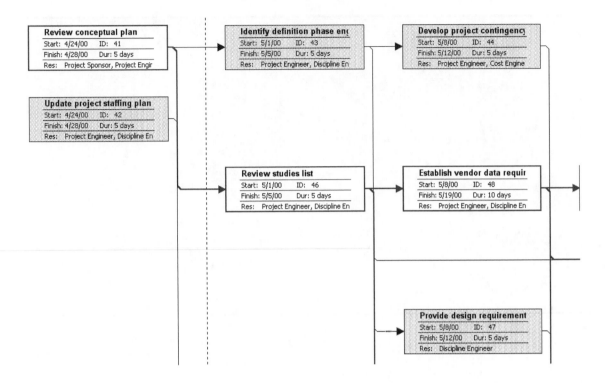

49

Worksheet 21. Network Diagram for Project[*]

---

[*] Part of the official project plan.

Resource Availability

At this point in the project planning process, all resources have been identified, approved, and procured. You know who is to be on your team and what equipment and materials you are acquiring to achieve project goals. In today's business climate, it's rare for people to be assigned to one project from start to finish with no additional responsibilities outside the scope of a single project. Sharing resources with other areas of the organization or among several projects requires careful resource management to ensure that the resource will be available to your project when it is needed.

Calendars

Project and resource calendars identify periods when work is possible. *Project calendars* affect all resources (e.g., some projects are 24/7, while others work only during normal business hours). *Resource calendars* affect a particular resource (e.g., a team member's personal schedule) or category of resources (e.g., work allowed by a union agreement). The availability of a work resource throughout the project can be specified in a number of ways:

- Set the work resource's working days and times.
    - What is the normal workweek for the resource?
    - Scheduled time off (vacations, travel, holidays, etc.)
    - Available substitutes
- Specify a work resource's starting and ending dates for the project.
- Specify a work resource's varying unit availability throughout the project. E.g., is the resource available to the project 100% of the time for some period and 50% for other periods?

Resource availability is commonly shown on a resource calendar. This is simply an ordinary calendar that has additional information about when the resource will be available for project work. Computer groupware programs such as Lotus Notes™ or Microsoft Exchange™ allow people to share their calendar information with others. Calendars for other resources or for people who do not have access to groupware can be constructed manually and included in the project planner.

When compiling work calendars, be sure to allow adequate lead and lag times for the resource. For example, a key person may agree to work on the project providing she is given at least a week's notice so she can reallocate her other work. Or there may be a two-week lag from the time a piece of equipment is ordered until it is delivered, set up, and ready to use. A place is provided in the Appendix for resource calendars (p. 211).

Figure 14. Example of a Computer-Generated Human Resource Calendar

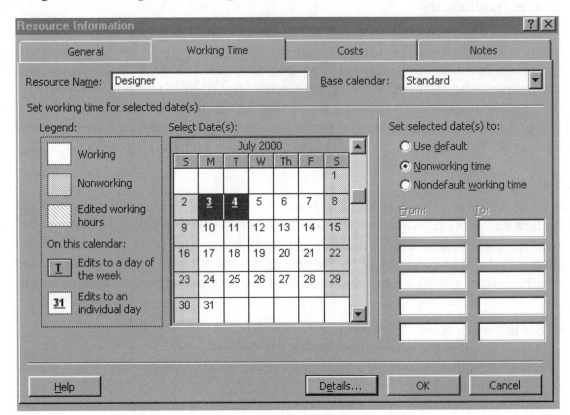

Worksheet 22. Resource Availability Information

Resource	Calendar Location	Issue #

53

Schedule Improvement

It is vital that the initial schedule not be accepted as a given. The information obtained in preparing the schedule can be used to improve the project schedule. Activities that the analysis indicates to be critical (i.e., those that lie on the critical path) are candidates for improvement. Pareto analysis can be used to identify those critical elements that are most likely to lead to significant improvement in overall project completion time. Cost data can be used to supplement the time data and the combined time/cost information can be analyzed using Pareto analysis. Be aware that the critical path may change when improvements are made. When this occurs, activities on the new critical path must be analyzed to see if new improvement opportunities appear.

The Importance of the Critical Path

The figure below is a reproduction of a figure presented earlier (see Figure 13—Example of a Computer-Generated Network Diagram, p. 49), except the figure below shows only those activities that lie on the critical path. These activities are examined first, because *any* improvement in these activities will make the project more likely to meet its target completion date. This happens because:

1. If the activity remains on the critical path after its cycle time has been reduced, it will result in reduced cycle time for the project.

2. If the activity comes off the critical path, it represents one less zero-slack activity subject to Murphy's Law.[15]

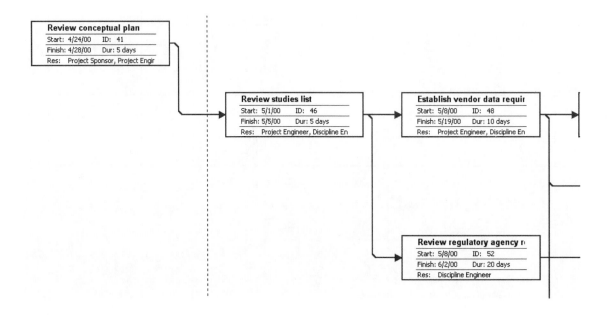

---

[15] Murphy's Law states that anything that can go wrong will.

Worksheet 23. Schedule Improvement Evaluation

Critical Activity Candidate	Ways to Shorten	Estimated Time Saved	Probability of Success	Expected Time Saved[16]	Issue #

---

[16] Expected time saved = estimated time saved X probability of saving this time.

Evaluating Uncertainty

Because projects involve the future, their paths are always uncertain. It is common to find that unanticipated events lead to project delays, cost overruns, quality problems, and even outright failure.

One way to deal with uncertainty and avoid unpleasant outcomes is to conduct *what-if analysis* to allow the team to anticipate and plan for likely future events. What-if analysis can also help the team improve project performance by manipulating the future to create situations beneficial to project success. For example, a key person might be persuaded to reschedule a vacation that occurs at a critical time in the project. The task list, project schedule, and analytical charts (Gantt, milestone, and network charts) completed above provide you with tools that can be used to explore various project scenarios and options. For example:

- What if our project had first priority for all of the resources? (This is known as "crash analysis.")

- What if the work calendar of a key resource were rearranged?

- What if a particular resource isn't available when the project needs it?

In this part of the project plan, the project team will review the project plan's robustness. That is, team members will evaluate the sensitivity of the plan to changing circumstances. The information obtained will be used to modify the project plan in ways that make it less likely to "break" as the future unfolds in various ways.

Variable Activity, Path, and Project Duration

Actually, the team already has some important information on uncertainty: the activity duration estimates obtained earlier. The optimistic, most likely, and pessimistic estimates differ from one another precisely because the people who provided the estimates were uncertain of the future. This information was used above to calculate *weighted averages*, which are statistical estimates of the expected duration of a given activity. However, there is addition information embedded in these estimates that will allow us to develop statistical probability distributions for the various paths as well as for the overall project schedule. The worksheet that follows will help you prepare variability estimates for the overall project.

Example of Evaluating Duration Estimates

A simple project consists of only seven tasks, with the estimated durations shown in the table below.

Activity	Depends On	Duration Estimates			Weighted Average[17]	Variance[18]	Sigma[19]
		(a) Optimistic	(b) Most Likely	(c) Pessimistic			
A		1	2	3	2.00	0.11	0.33
B	A	3	5	9	5.33	1.00	1.00
C	B	2	8	14	8.00	4.00	2.00
D	C	1	6	13	6.33	4.00	2.00
E	B	1	3	7	3.33	1.00	1.00
F	E	3	4	8	4.50	0.69	0.83
G	D, F	2	6	11	6.17	2.25	1.50

The network chart for this project is shown below. The critical path (using the most likely duration estimates) is indicated as a solid line.

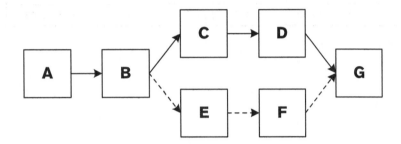

There are several ways in which this information can be analyzed. For example, we could compare the schedules that result from assuming that a given set of durations is correct. The results of this analysis are presented in the table below. This analysis provides best-case, expected, and worst-case scenarios. For the example, the project is scheduled to begin on March 31, 2003. The best-case finish would be April 11, 2003. The two expected finishes are May 7 (based on the weighted averages) or May 6 (using the most likely duration estimates). The worst-case finish would be June 6. These estimates can be compared to the project's target due date and used for planning. The optimistic analysis can be used in crash schedule planning[20] or the pessimistic analysis can be used for evaluating the effect of shifting resources to higher-priority projects.

---

[17] Weighted average = (a + 4b + c) / 6.

[18] Variance = [(c - a) / 6]^2.

[19] Sigma = [(c - a) / 6].

[20] See "Calculating the Cost of a Schedule," p. 66.

Weighted Average Schedule

Task	Duration	Start	End
A	2d	Mon 3/31/03	Tue 4/1/03
B	5.33d	Wed 4/2/03	Wed 4/9/03
C	8d	Wed 4/9/03	Mon 4/21/03
D	6.33d	Mon 4/21/03	Tue 4/29/03
E	3.33d	Wed 4/9/03	Mon 4/14/03
F	4.5d	Mon 4/14/03	Mon 4/21/03
G	6.17d	Tue 4/29/03	Wed 5/7/03

Most Likely Schedule

Task	Duration	Start	End
A	2d	Mon 3/31/03	Tue 4/1/03
B	5d	Wed 4/2/03	Tue 4/8/03
C	8d	Wed 4/9/03	Fri 4/18/03
D	6d	Mon 4/21/03	Mon 4/28/03
E	3d	Wed 4/9/03	Fri 4/11/03
F	4d	Mon 4/14/03	Thu 4/17/03
G	6d	Tue 4/29/03	Tue 5/6/03

Optimistic Schedule

Task	Duration	Start	End
A	1d	Mon 3/31/03	Mon 3/31/03
B	3d	Tue 4/1/03	Thu 4/3/03
C	2d	Fri 4/4/03	Mon 4/7/03
D	1d	Tue 4/8/03	Tue 4/8/03
E	1d	Fri 4/4/03	Fri 4/4/03
F	3d	Mon 4/7/03	Wed 4/9/03
G	2d	Thu 4/10/03	Fri 4/11/03

Pessimistic Schedule

Task	Duration	Start	End
A	3d	Mon 3/31/03	Wed 4/2/03
B	9d	Thu 4/3/03	Tue 4/15/03
C	14d	Wed 4/16/03	Mon 5/5/03
D	13d	Tue 5/6/03	Thu 5/22/03
E	7d	Wed 4/16/03	Thu 4/24/03
F	8d	Fri 4/25/03	Tue 5/6/03
G	11d	Fri 5/23/03	Fri 6/6/03

Worksheet 24. Best-Case, Expected, and Worst-Case Schedule Completion Dates

Task	Completion Date Duration Estimates			
	Best Case	Weighted Average	Most Likely	Worst Case

Estimating Project Duration Statistically

While useful, the above analysis is missing some important information, namely probabilities associated with each schedule. We know for example that the best- and worst-case scenarios are combinations of improbable events and are therefore extremely unlikely. These estimates provide useful bounds for our schedule estimates and are helpful in determining whether or not the deadline is even realistic, but it would be even better if we established a statistical distribution of schedule completion dates. We will do so now.

Consider the schedule information in the table below, which is an excerpt from the table used in the previous example. You may wish to review the diagram presented earlier to confirm that critical path is A-B-C-D-G and the noncritical path is A-B-E-F-G. The activities in gray cells are not on the critical path.

Activity	Activity Duration		
	Mean	Variance	Sigma
A	2.00	0.11	0.33
B	5.33	1.00	1.00
C	8.00	4.00	2.00
D	6.33	4.00	2.00
E	3.33	1.00	1.00
F	4.50	0.69	0.83
G	6.17	2.25	1.50

From these data it is possible to compute the mean, variance, and standard deviation for the critical and noncritical paths. The path mean is the sum of the activity means (we are using the weighted averages here), the path variance is the sum of the variances of the activities on the path, and the path standard deviation is the square root of the path variance. For these data we get the following statistical estimates:

Path	Mean	Variance	Sigma
ABCDG	27.83	11.36	3.370625
ABEDF	21.33	5.06	2.248456

Statistically, due to the central limit theorem, the sum of five or more distributions will usually be approximately normally distributed. Thus, for the critical path (and for the project), the time to our scheduled completion date can be considered to be approximately normally distributed, with a mean time to completion of 27.83 working days and a standard deviation of 3.4 working days. Reviewing the calendar for this project, scheduled to begin on Monday, March 31, 2003, we see that (assuming resource availability) this would mean that the project is expected to finish on May 8. A 95% confidence interval (expected completion date ±2 sigma, or ±7 days) for schedule completion would be from April 24 to May 23. Note that this interval is much tighter than that obtained in the best-case/worst-case analysis.[21]

Probability of Meeting Project Due Date

With the information we now have, it is possible to calculate the probability that the project will be completed on or before its due date. This is done by calculating the Z statistic using the due date and the calculated schedule mean and standard deviation. The calculations are shown below:

$$Z = \frac{\text{Due date duration - Project mean duration}}{\text{Project sigma}} \qquad \text{(Equation 1)}$$

For example, assume that the project due date is Friday, May 16 for a project due date duration of 34 workdays. This gives

$$Z = \frac{34 - 27.83}{3.37} = 1.83$$

The area of a standard normal curve below $z = 1.83$ is 96.6%. Assuming that the duration estimates are correct, this is the probability of meeting the project due date.

Note: The MS Excel function for the cumulative standard normal distribution is =NORMDIST(Z,0,1,TRUE). In our example, $z = 1.83$, so the function becomes =NORMDIST(1.83,0,1,TRUE).

---

[21] Note: If your project has multiple critical paths, or if the 95% confidence interval for a noncritical path extends beyond the confidence interval for the critical path, project schedule estimates should be based on the path that gives the longest completion time estimates.

Worksheet 25. Statistical Analysis of Project Duration

Path	Mean	Variance	Sigma	Lower 95% Estimate	Upper 95% Estimate

Project Due Date	
Expected Project Completion Date	
Standard Deviation of Project Completion	
95% Lower Confidence Interval (expected completion date minus two standard deviations)	
95% Upper Confidence Interval (expected completion date plus two standard deviations)	
Probability of Meeting Due Date	

If the probability of not meeting the due date is high, the deadline should be discussed with the project sponsor. In some cases it is necessary to modify the project's charter, assign additional resources, etc.

Using Simulation to Analyze Project Schedules

The analysis conducted above involves a number of simplifying assumptions and approximations. In most cases, the accuracy of the results will be more than adequate. However, it is possible to conduct a more precise analysis using computer simulation. The example here uses the program Crystal Ball® (CB).[22]

---

[22] Available from Decisioneering, Inc., www.decisioneering.com.

In the earlier example, the calculations assumed that the task durations could be modeled using the beta distribution. If, during the historical analysis phase, we located sufficient data on similar tasks, we would not have needed to make this assumption. Instead, we could use software to determine the best-fit statistical distribution for each task. However, if historical data are not available, we can still use CB to model our project schedule using the duration estimates. In the figure below, data are entered for activity A, assuming that optimistic = 0.1% probability, most likely = 50%, and pessimistic = 99.9%. CB will use a beta distribution with these parameters in the simulation. (A wide variety of other distributions could also be used.) Data for other activities were entered in a similar manner.

Figure 15. Computer Screen for Entering Task Duration Data

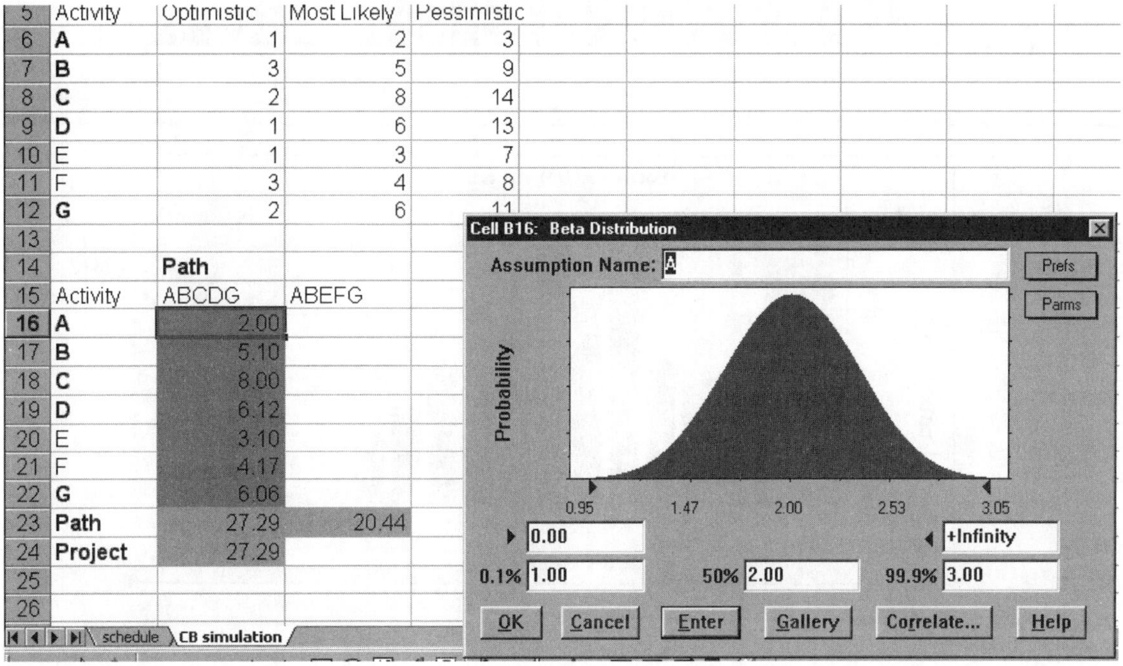

Project duration is defined in the spreadsheet as the maximum of the critical or the noncritical path duration. CB runs as many simulations as desired; for the example, 1,000 project schedules were simulated. The results are shown in Figure 16.

Figure 16. Results of Simulation for Example

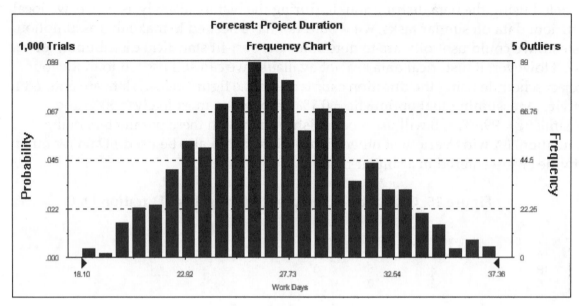

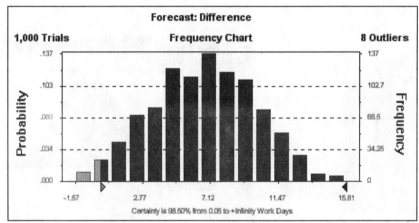

Discussion of Results

As expected, the distribution of project completion times appears to be approximately normal. The mean and range of results are also quite close to what we obtained from the statistical estimates. However, the simulation allows us to quickly explore a variety of questions. For example, the second chart in Figure 16 shows us that the critical path is not always the critical path! This chart is a histogram of the difference between the critical path and the so-called noncritical path. It can be seen that about 1.5% of the time the difference is negative, indicating that the noncritical path took longer to complete than the critical path. This has obvious project management implications, such as not to ignore tasks that are not on the critical path.

The ease of asking such what-if questions is a major benefit of simulation software. In addition, many people (even some project sponsors!) are unfamiliar with statistics: assumptions, such as the approximate normality of project durations, make th .n uneasy. For these people, simulation can serve as a valuable confirmation of these assumptions. The truth is, more than a few statisticians breathe a sigh of relief when simulation results match analytical predictions.

The simulation can be used to answer other questions as well. For example, the probability of the project being completed by its 34-day due date is shown in Figure 17. The simulation prediction of 95.9% probability of success is very close to the 96.6% predicted by the analytical approach used earlier.

Figure 17. Simulation Results: Probability of Meeting Due Date

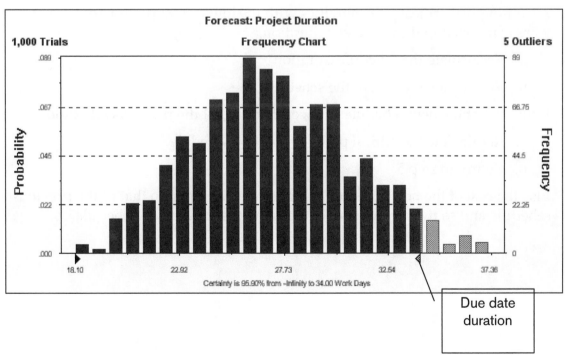

Calculating the Cost of a Schedule

The cost of following a particular schedule should be evaluated carefully. It often happens that a cost savings can be achieved by using a schedule other than the schedule based on the most likely or weighted average duration estimates. As activity durations are compressed, the time it takes to complete the project will decline, while the *direct costs* of completing the project will *increase*. Conversely, *indirect costs* such as overhead generally *decrease* when projects take less time to complete. When the indirect costs are added to the direct costs, total costs will tend to decline to a minimum for a particular schedule, which we will call a *cost-optimized schedule*.

Identifying a cost-optimized schedule involves these steps:[23]

1. Ask those assigned to each activity to estimate the direct and indirect costs of completing their activity in the duration of the optimistic, most likely, and pessimistic estimates.

2. Create a spreadsheet of the above cost and time estimates.

3. Compute the total cost of the schedule, including direct and indirect costs.

4. Create a column showing the cost per unit of time saved for each activity. E.g., if an activity can be completed in four weeks at a cost of $2000 or in two weeks at a cost of $4000, then the cost per week saved is $1000.

5. Rank-order the activities in ascending order by cost per unit of time saved, i.e., put the lowest cost per unit of time saved at the top of the list and the highest cost per unit of time saved at the bottom of the list.

6. Assuming that critical path activities with the lowest cost per unit of time saved were completed in the optimistic duration,

   a. Recalculate the schedule duration.

   b. Recalculate the cost of the schedule.

7. If the cost of the new schedule is lower than that of the previous schedule,

   a. Recalculate the critical path for the new schedule.

   b. Return to step 5.

   Else the cost of the new schedule is higher than or equal to that of the previous schedule and so the previous schedule is the cost-optimized schedule.

---

[23] See Worksheets 27 and 28, pp. 68 and 69, for analysis details.

Worksheet 26. Estimated Cost by Activity Duration

Activity	Responsibility	Cost to Complete by Duration Estimate		
		Optimistic	Most Likely	Pessimistic

Worksheet 27. Cost-Optimization Spreadsheet Results[24]

---

[24] Insert spreadsheet or table showing total cost by schedule.

Worksheet 28. Cost-Optimization Graphical Analysis[25]

---

[25] Insert graph showing total cost by schedule.

Resource Leveling

Resource leveling is a way to resolve having too much work assigned to resources, a situation known as *resource over-allocation*. One way to level is to delay an activity until the assigned resource has time to work on it. Another method is to split an activity, so that part of an activity is done when planned and the rest of it is done later, when the assigned resource has time. Resource leveling is a vital part of project schedule development and validation.

When leveling resources, you should examine the following factors to determine which activities should be delayed or split:

- Available slack time
- Activity priority
- Activity dependencies
- Activity constraints (e.g., must start on date, must finish on date)
- Scheduled dates for activity

When leveling resources, one generally does not change resource assignments or activity information. Resource leveling usually only delays or splits activities. The methods you choose to reduce over-allocations depend on the limitations of your project, including budget, resource availability, project due date, and the degree of flexibility available for scheduling activities.

Worksheet 29. Resource Leveling

Activity	Slack	Dependencies or Constraints	Scheduled Dates	Over-allocated Resource	Leveling Strategy	Issue #

Project Control Subplans

Project control subplans can be developed for five major areas: risk, quality, cost, schedule, and scope. Blank sheets are provided in the Appendix to include information on each of these subplans. Unlike the plans that deal with creating the project's deliverables, these subplans focus on the mechanics of managing the project. Although their impact on the deliverables is indirect, the impact of these subplans on the success of the project should not be underestimated. Projects routinely fail to produce the expected deliverables due to unanticipated risk or uncontrolled scope creep or scope drift. Equally common are projects that produce deliverables that don't meet the expectations or needs of the project's stakeholders. Finally, projects that produce the desired deliverable but take too long or cost too much must also be judged as less than completely successful in meeting their goals and objectives.

Risk Control Plan[*]

Because projects deal with the future, all projects involve risk. The basic risk considered by the risk control plan is that of the project not meeting its overall goals and objectives. Separate control subplans deal with risks involving quality, cost, and schedule.

Resilience

It is worth noting that there are two ways of dealing with risk: anticipation and resilience. Our focus will be on anticipating risk and preparing plans to avoid or mitigate risk, but you should be aware of the resilience option.

Resilience is the ability to achieve your goals *despite* the impact of unanticipated risk. Resilience is related to robustness. Robustness is the capacity of the project plan to succeed in the face of normal variability, while resilience is the ability to produce at least a partially successful result even when the future is radically different than expected.

One way of thinking about resilience is that it is the ability to "turn on a dime," to pull together the pieces of potential failure and move in an entirely different direction, or, similarly, to recognize a better opportunity and quickly redirect the project's resources to take advantage of it. Resilience is seeing that your bacteria culture experiment was ruined by an unknown mold and then recognizing the potential of penicillin.

---

[*] Part of the official project plan.

72

The risk control plan addresses four areas:

1. Identifying the risk
2. Measuring the risk
3. Preparing risk response plans
4. Executing the risk response plans

Identifying and Measuring the Risk

As the name implies, the first step is to recognize which risks are likely to affect the project. Once identified, these risks will be described in clear and concise terms to ensure that all team members understand them. This activity, by itself, will go a long way toward mitigating the risk. Often, simply by seeing a risk, team members will spot flaws in their project plan that they can address immediately. The project team may wish to brainstorm to develop a list of potential risks. Examples are:

- *What adverse events have affected other projects in this organization in the past?*

    – Similar projects

    – Any project

    The team may wish to interview team members who have participated in other projects. This question could also be included in the interviews conducted during the activity definition phase. If your organization has an online database of projects, you may find information there. You may also wish to search the Web or Usenet discussion groups. (www.google.com contains searchable archives of newsgroup discussions.)

- *What new technology must we develop or use to successfully complete this project?*

    Projects that use proven technologies are inherently less risky than those that rely on state-of-the-art technology. Riskier still are those that require innovation and invention for success. Creativity is still impossible to program.

- *How reliable are the cost, duration estimates, scope elements, and other inputs on which the project plan is based?*

    There's an old saying in the computer science field, "Garbage in, garbage out" (GIGO). Your project's action plan was developed based on the inputs from a wide variety of sources. Now is the time to step back and ask whether any of those inputs might be of questionable accuracy or reliability. We are *not* implying that any of the people providing information are incompetent or deceitful. Rather, we are saying that some inputs are inherently more difficult to know with certainty than others. For example, activity duration estimates based on historical experience with a dozen similar projects are more trustworthy than estimates based on the recollection of an individual from a project he worked on several years ago. Focus on activity estimates that, if wrong, will have a significant impact on the project's ability to deliver as promised.

- *What is the likelihood that key people will be removed from the project before it is completed?*

  Loss of a key individual may deal the project a significant blow. For example, if the project's sponsor is promoted, is transferred, or leaves for any other reason, the project will be without the single individual with complete responsibility for the value stream. Loss of key technical personnel from the team or from assignments can also have an adverse impact. The team may wish to prepare a list of those on the project who have unique skills and for whom there is no known replacement.

- *What is the likelihood of a significant reorganization occurring during the project?*

  If a new leader has recently taken over the organization where the project is being conducted, consider the chances that a major restructuring might take place. Mergers and acquisitions are another common reason for reorganizations. The purpose of this question isn't to cause team members to fret over job security, but to provide input for contingency planning. Since Six Sigma projects focus on value streams rather than functional areas, a major reorganization may have little effect on the chances of success, but the need to consult with new stakeholders may arise.

- *How might external market conditions impact the project?*

  What is the condition of the market for the organization, its key customers, and its key suppliers? How would a loss of business impact the project? New business? Loss of a key supplier? New suppliers?

- *Have new opportunities materialized since the inception of the project?*

  In preparing the project plan, the team explores many different areas, including best practices, optimal performance levels, knowledge discovery, etc. Often the exercise of developing a project plan results in insights that can develop into new products or processes, new markets for the organization's products or services, identification of new technologies, etc. These opportunities should be documented and communicated to others in the organization. If the team or its members are asked to pursue these opportunities, what will happen to the project?

The number of possible questions is endless. The team should brainstorm to identify as many questions as possible. After brainstorming, the team will explore the likely effects of the risk events on the project. There are a number of tools the team can use in making this determination.

Table 3. Tools Useful in Risk Assessment

Risk Assessment Tool[26]
❏ Check sheets
❏ Pareto analysis
❏ Cause-and-effect diagram
❏ Interrelationship digraphs
❏ Prioritization matrices
❏ Force field analysis
❏ Failure Mode and Effect Analysis (FMEA)
❏ Fault Tree Analysis (FTA)

Risk events will be classified according to the impact on the project and the likelihood of occurring. Planning requirements based on this classification are shown in the following table:

Table 4. Risk Planning vs. Impact and Likelihood of Threatening Events

Likelihood	Impact on Project Success		
	Very Serious	Moderately Serious	Not Serious
Highly Likely	Detailed plan	Basic plan	No plan necessary
Likely	Detailed plan	Basic plan	No plan necessary
Not Very Likely	Basic plan	No plan necessary	No plan necessary

Detailed risk plans will include specifying triggers that will activate the action, in-depth analysis of the threat posed, specific actions that will be taken to avoid or mitigate the risk, etc. Basic risk plans will include how the risky situation is to be monitored and who will be responsible for responding if the threat materializes.

Use Worksheet 30 to document and classify each risk event.

---

[26] *Six Sigma Handbook,* Chapters 8 and 16.

Worksheet 30. Risk Event Classification

Likelihood	Impact on Project Success		
	Very Serious	Moderately Serious	Not Serious
Highly Likely			
Likely			
Not Very Likely			

Worksheet 31. New Opportunities

List the opportunities discovered by the project team and who will be notified of these opportunities.

Opportunity	Person Informed of Opportunity

Risk Response Planning

Risk response plans should be prepared for those risk events identified as having a high likelihood/impact profile. The tools shown in Table 5. Risk Response Planning Tools can help the team with risk response planning. In addition, the team should also review the results of its risk assessment for risk planning ideas. Risk assessments show the team where the risk "lever points" are. Response plans can take advantage of this information by indicating where the team should focus its response.

Table 5. Risk Response Planning Tools

Risk Response Planning Tool[27]
Force Field Analysis
Process decision program charts
FMEA

---

[27] *Six Sigma Handbook,* Chapters 8 and 16.

Worksheet 32. Risk Response Plans

Risk Event	Response Plan Location[28]	Responsibility

---

[28] E.g., network document, person, binder, etc.

Quality Plan[*]

The output from the quality plan activity is the project quality plan. A quality plan is a document setting out the specific quality practices, resources and sequences of activities relevant to a particular project or deliverable. According to the Project Management Institute, project quality management

> includes the processes required to ensure that the project will satisfy the needs for which it was undertaken. It includes all activities of the overall management function that determine the quality policy, objectives, and responsibilities and implements them by means such as quality planning, quality control, quality assurance, and quality improvement, within the quality system.[29]

- *Quality planning* involves identifying which quality standards are relevant to the project and preparing plans that will satisfy the requirements.

- *Quality control* (QC) is the appraisal of specific project outcomes to determine if they comply with quality requirements and taking corrective action if noncompliance is found.

- *Quality assurance* (QA) is the periodic review of actual project performance to ensure that quality plans have been implemented and that quality procedures are being followed correctly. QA also involves taking corrective action if noncompliance with established procedures is found or modifying the quality plan if QC results show that it is inadequate.

As can be seen, the quality plan addresses the project's processes as well as the project's deliverables. However, due to the nature of Six Sigma, Six Sigma projects have a built-in concern for quality issues. Indeed, the *Planner* integrates product quality measurement into the project plan completely. Thus, the "Quality Plan" section in the *Planner* will be concerned primarily with project and deliverable quality issues rather than with product or service quality issues. The team should keep in mind that all of the tools and techniques used to create quality products can be used to provide project and deliverable quality.

Quality Planning

To prepare for the creation of the quality plan the team must review information from a number of sources, including:

- The organization's quality policy and, if available, its quality manual

- The project charter and the Project Charter Form

---

[*] Part of the official project plan.

[29] Duncan, William R. (1996). *A Guide to the Project Management Body of Knowledge.* Newtown Square, PA: Project Management Institute.

- The deliverables description and the metrics used to validate the deliverables
- Standards and regulations that affect the project
- Other areas of the project plan, as applicable

In the section of the *Planner* entitled "How Will I Measure Project Success?" (p. 18), project deliverables are listed along with the metrics used to validate the quality of each deliverable and the frequency of measurement. The quality plan should operationally define these metrics and provide a system for measuring them and recording the results. Also, the section entitled "How Will I Monitor Satisfaction with Project Progress?" (p. 22) lists several project quality metrics that are to be monitored during project execution.

Worksheet 33. Quality Plan Items

Quality Plan Item	Means of Monitoring	Report Distribution	Frequency	Quality Plan Reference
Quality Issues: open, closed, % closed per week or month, new issues per week or month	Written report, c chart			
DPMO vs. a checklist of criteria	c chart			
Quality judgments on intermediate project deliverables by someone qualified to make the judgments (must be defined operationally)	Written report			
Project satisfaction survey results: sponsors, customers, team members, others	p chart of % giving high or low ratings, X-bar/s chart of scored items			
Intermediate improvement of key business metrics to date vs. baseline—e.g., reduced defect rates, improved process time, increased customer satisfaction with product or service quality, reduced costs, improved process capability	Written report, descriptive statistics			
Results of WBS reintegration tests	Written report			
Project change requests	Change control plan			

Quality Plan Item	Means of Monitoring	Report Distribution	Frequency	Quality Plan Reference

Cost Control Plan[*]

The project manager must know where he or she stands in terms of expenditures. Once the manager is informed that a given amount of future expense is allocated to him or her for a particular project, it is his or her job to run the project so that this allowance is not exceeded. The process of allocating resources to be expended in the future is called *budgeting*. Budgets should be viewed as forecasts of future events; in this case, the events are expenditures. A listing of these expenditures, broken out into specific categories, is called the *budget*. Project budgets are commonly prepared for the following categories of expenses:

- *Direct labor budgets* are usually prepared for each work element in the project plan, then aggregated for the project as a whole. Control is usually maintained at the work element level to ensure that the aggregate budget allowance is not exceeded. Budgets may be in terms of dollars or some other measure of value, such as direct labor hours expended.

- *Support services budgets* need to be prepared, because without budgets support services tend to charge based on actuals, without allowances for errors, rework, etc. The discipline imposed by making budget estimates and being held to them often leads to improved efficiency and higher quality.

- *Purchased items budgets* covers purchased materials, equipment, and services. The budgets can be based on negotiated or market prices. The issues mentioned for support services also apply here.

Budget Reports

Budgets allocate resources to be used in the future. No one can predict the future with certainty. Thus, an important element in the budgeting process is tracking actual expenditures after the budgets have been prepared. The following techniques are useful in monitoring actual expenditures vs. budgeted expenditures.

- *Expenditure reports* that compare actual expenditures with budgeted expenditures are periodically submitted to the budget authority, e.g., finance, sponsor.

- *Expenditure audits* are conducted to verify that charges to the project are legitimate and that the work charged for was actually performed. In most large organizations with multiple projects in work at any given time, it is possible to find projects being charged for work done on other projects, for work not yet done, etc. While these charges are often inadvertent, in fairness to the various sponsors they must still be identified and controlled.

- *Variance reporting* compares actual expenditures with budgeted expenditures directly. The term *variance* is used here in the accounting sense, not the statistical sense. In accounting, a variance is simply a comparison of a planned amount

---

[*] Part of the official project plan.

with an actual amount. An accounting variance may or may not indicate a special cause of variation; statistical techniques are required to make this determination. The timing of variance reporting varies depending on the need for control. The timing of variance reports should be determined in advance and written into the project plan.

- *Variance tables:* Variance reports can appear in a variety of formats. Most common are simple tables that show the actual/budgeted/variances by budget item and overall for the current period and cumulatively for the project. Since it is unlikely that variances will be zero, an allowance is usually made, e.g., 5% over or under is allowed without the need for explanations.

- *Control charts:* For longer projects, historical actuals can be plotted on control charts and used to set allowances.

- *Variance graphs:* When only tables are used, it is difficult to spot patterns. To remedy this problem, tables are often supplemented with graphs. Graphs generally show the budget variances in a time-ordered sequence on a line chart. The allowance lines calculated from control charts can be drawn on the graph to provide a visual guide to the eye.

Worksheet 34. Project Budget Reports and Reporting Frequency

Report Type	Report Name	Frequency	Responsibility	Issue #
Expenditures				
Expenditure Audits				
Variances				
Control Chart				

Analysis of Budget Reports

The project manager and Black Belt should review the variance data for patterns that contain useful information. Ideally, the pattern will be a mixture of positive and negative but economically and statistically insignificant variances. Assuming that this pattern is accompanied by an on-schedule project, this indicates a reasonably good budget, i.e., an accurate forecasting of expenditures. Variances should be evaluated separately for each type of budget (direct labor, materials, etc.). However, the variance report for the entire project is the primary source of information concerning the status of the project in terms of resource use. Reports are received and analyzed periodically. For most quality improvement projects, monthly or weekly reports are adequate. Budget variance analysis[30] should include the following:

- *Trends*: Occasional departures from budget are to be expected. Of greater concern is a pattern that indicates a fundamental problem with the budget. Trends are easier to detect from graphic reports.

- *Overspending*: Since budgeted resources are generally scarce, overspending represents a serious threat to the project and, perhaps, to the organization itself. When a project overspends its budget, it depletes the resources available for other activities and projects. The project team, team leader, and sponsors should design monitoring systems to detect and correct overspending quickly. Overspending is often a symptom of other problems with the project, e.g., paying extra in an attempt to catch up after falling behind schedule, additional expenses for rework, etc.

- *Underspending* is potentially as serious a problem as overspending. If the project budget was prepared properly, then the expenses reflect a given schedule and quality level. Underspending may reflect "cutting corners" or allowing suppliers an allowance for slower delivery. The reasons for any significant departure from the plan should be explained. If the underspending is justified, the project manager should report the situation to the project sponsor at once so that resources can be redirected to other enterprise priorities.

Schedule Control Plan[*]

The primary means of controlling the project's schedule are periodic progress reviews and timely response to deviations from schedule. Of course, the foundation of this activity is an accurate schedule and ongoing commitment to the project on the part of those involved. Should a pattern of schedule slippages appear and remain uncorrected, the project manager must call it to the attention of the project sponsor quickly enough to save the project delivery date.

---

[30] This is not to be confused with the statistical technique, Analysis of Variance (ANOVA).

[*] Part of the official project plan.

Project Schedule Management

The *Planner* will provide two alternatives for project schedule management. The traditional approach is to focus on individual activities. A relatively new approach, called the *critical chain approach*, focuses on the project and the organization's portfolio of projects as integrated systems. Both methods have their proponents (and opponents) and both are presented here. In all likelihood, the Six Sigma project team will be required to follow the system practiced by its organization.

Traditional project schedule management involves a focus on *activities*. Status reports are prepared by those responsible for the various activities. For each activity, these reports include percentage completion, expected completion date, issues and plans to overcome them, etc. Activity-based action plans are set in motion when activities are substantially beyond their expected completion dates. The premise of this approach to schedule management is that if activities are carefully monitored, the project due date will take care of itself.

Worksheet 35. Activity Status Management Report

Activity	Critical Path?	Responsibility	Report Date	Percent Complete	Projected Completion Date	Issue #

Scope Change Control Plan[*]

Project scope management describes the processes required to ensure that the project includes all the work required and only the work required to complete the project successfully. It consists of initiation, scope planning, scope definition, scope verification, and scope change control (Duncan, 1996, page 6). This section of *The Six Sigma Project Planner* addresses scope change control; the other subjects addressed by scope management are covered in earlier sections of the *Planner*.

The scope change control plan addresses how scope changes will be identified, classified, and integrated into the project. Scope change almost always involves either *scope creep* (the tendency for a project's scope to grow beyond the original scope) or *scope drift* (the tendency for a project's scope to change unintentionally over time). Scope creep diverts resources from the project's authorized scope. Both scope creep and scope drift create a lack of focus on the project's authorized goals and deliverables. These are serious issues for the project team; project failure due to poor scope change control is very common.

Inputs to the scope change control plan include:

- Project charter (pp. 2-3)
- WBS (p. 29)
- Issues lists (Appendix, p. 200, Worksheet 71)
- Quality plan items (p. 80)
- Budget reports (pp. 84-85)
- Project schedule (p. 49)
- Change requests (p. 206)

The team should review the above documents before creating the scope change control plan. The outputs of this activity are the scope change control plan, scope change reports, and corrective action. The change control plan should include periodic review of activity audit reports, issues lists, performance reports (quality, cost, and schedule), and change requests.

Change Control System

The *Project Management Body of Knowledge* defines a change control system as:
> "A collection of formal, documented procedures that defines the steps by which official project documents may be changed. It includes the paperwork, tracking systems, and approval levels necessary for authorizing changes."

In developing change control systems, project teams are advised to look to their organization's own policies and procedures for guidance. Nearly all but the smallest organizations have systems in place for ensuring that policy and procedure changes are

---

[*] Part of the official project plan.

90

viewed and approved by the proper personnel. Product configuration and drawing change control systems are virtually universal in manufacturing organizations and project teams may find a complete system, or at least a good template, in their organization's quality manual. Documented and implemented change control systems are an ISO 9000 requirement.

Elements of Change Control Systems

For those who do not have access to a documented change control system, here's a checklist that can be used to develop a simple system.

- As a general rule, *the project team should develop the least restrictive system that will ensure proper control of the project's major documents.* For many Six Sigma projects, this will be a very simple and straightforward system.

- Identify the control point—a key individual who will be the custodian of the official version of the official project plan. This person will have password-protected access to any electronic master documents.

- How are change requests submitted? Which forms are to be used? To whom are they submitted for approval?

- Change requests should always include a "reason for change" section. Information from this section should be reviewed periodically to identify systemic problems and opportunities for improvement.

- What will ensure that change requests are considered in a timely fashion?

- How will the requestor be notified of the disposition of his or her change requests?

- The team should review the planner and list those documents in the planner that will be subject to formal change control. Include only those documents for which change control is truly necessary. (Note: Items in the *Planner* marked with an * are generally considered to be part of the official project plan and candidates for change control.)

- For each controlled document, identify which members of the organization and/or the project team will have the authority to approve a change.

- In very specific terms, describe how changes will be incorporated into the official plan. For example, are changes to be made to master documents using a particular word processor? Is a special font used to denote changes?

- How will changes be officially incorporated into the master documents?

- How and to whom will revisions be communicated?

- If multiple approvals are required, how is the change to be routed for approval? Is a single document to be sent sequentially or will multiple review copies go out simultaneously? How will comments from multiple reviewers be integrated into the master document?

- It is recommended that, if possible, the team have a single, read-only official electronic copy and all paper copies be considered "reference only." This should be so noted on printouts. Printouts should also bear the date and time printed and revision information.

- If paper copies are used, what will be done to ensure that obsolete documents are removed from use?

- Describe whether or not configuration management will be used. For our purpose here, configuration management is described as the maintenance of an audit trail to track each change, who made the change, and when it was made. Most modern word processing software can capture this information and store it with a document. For example, in MS Word one would turn on "track changes" before making changes, to capture the information.

Provision for Making Rapid Changes

It may happen that an immediate change is necessary and provision must be made to allow such changes. Change control systems routinely provide this flexibility. For example, one major aircraft manufacturer allows authorized engineers to change manufacturing plans by using a red pen to cross out incorrect information, writing the correct information on the working copy of the plan, initialing and dating the change, and noting the number of the formal change or deviation request form that ties the change to the formal planning change control system. Similar provisions should be made in the project's change control system. Of course, electronic equivalents can be used if necessary. Record detailed information in the "Project Change Control Plan" section of the Appendix, p. 206.

Worksheet 36. Change Control Information

Control Point Name	Phone	Pager	E-mail	Address

Alternate Name	Phone	Pager	E-mail	Address

Worksheet 37. Controlled Documents List

Chapter 2
Define

What Is the Current State?

In this section, a process map is created for the process or processes that the project will improve. Using the icons shown in Worksheet 38, draw a process map illustrating the current state of the business process being addressed by this project. How does the current process deliver value to the customer? What is the flow of the process? Be sure to include unplanned effects (e.g., scrap, complaints, delays) as well as planned effects. Use additional pages as required. The most commonly used symbols are shown.

Figure 18. Example of Cross-Functional Process Map

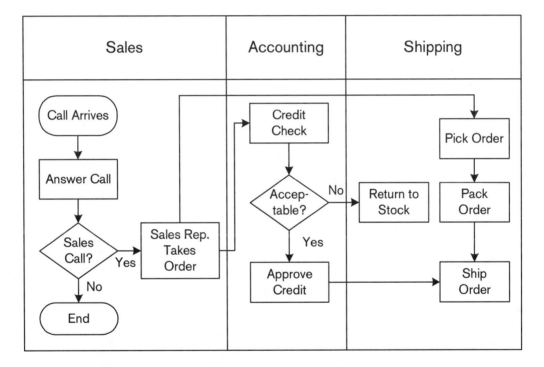

Note that the departments are shown across the top. It is just as common to show departments along the side of the diagram. Often diagrams are drawn showing both responsibilities (e.g., departments, people) and process phases (e.g., a timeline). For example, a map of a Six Sigma project might show Black Belt, Green Belt, Sponsor, and Team Member names along the side, and Define-Measure-Analyze-Improve-Control as project phases.

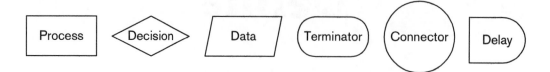

What's Wrong with the Way Things Are Now?

Describe the undesirable effects (UDEs, pronounced "you-dees") in narrative terms—e.g., "Customers are unhappy with our service because our wait times are too long" or "Repeat business is down dramatically since our cutbacks." List as many UDEs as you can think of.

Worksheet 39. Narrative Description of Undesirable Effects

Quantify the Undesirable Effects

Examples of quantifiable UDEs are:

- Customer dissatisfaction
- Customer complaints

Customer defections field returns

- Field repair
- Wait time
- Declining owner or shareholder equity
- Declining sales
- Losses
- Negative cash flow
- Excessive inventory levels
- Losses due to obsolescence
- High levels of accounts receivable
- Technical support
- Scrap losses
- Rework losses
- Total cycle time
- Non-value-added time
- Order entry errors
- Fulfillment errors
- Incomplete kits
- Total cost of poor quality

Tools and Techniques

In the Define phase, you need to determine which opportunities will provide the biggest payoff for our efforts. Part of this task involves describing the current state of various metrics. You are interested in learning how various metrics behave. Are there any important trends? Are the data relatively stable or are there outliers? What do the statistical distributions look like? Are the distributions what we'd expect from this process?

In addition to process mapping and flowcharting, some tools and techniques to consider during the Define phase include the following:

- Check sheets

- Pareto analysis

- Cause-and-effect diagrams

- Seven management tools for quality control (7M tools)

- Data mining: exploring information contained in the enterprise data warehouses using automated or semi-automated means

Worksheet 40. Undesirable Effects

Undesirable Effect	Mean or Median	Standard Deviation	In Statistical Control?

Failure Mode and Effect Analysis (FMEA)

Failure mode and effect analysis (FMEA) is an attempt to delineate every possible failure, its effects on the system, the likelihood of occurrence, and the probability that the failure will go undetected. FMEA provides an excellent basis for classification of characteristics, i.e., for identifying CTQs and other critical variables. As with Pareto analysis, one objective of FMEA is to direct the available resources toward the most promising opportunities. An extremely unlikely failure, even a failure with serious consequences, may not be the best place to concentrate preventive efforts. FMEA can be combined with decision analysis methods such as the analytic hierarchy process (AHP) and quality function deployment (QFD) to help guide preventive action planning.

FMEA came into existence in the space program in the 1960s. Later it was incorporated into military standards, in particular Mil-Std-1629A.[1] There are two primary approaches for accomplishing an FMEA:

- *The hardware approach,* which lists individual hardware items and analyzes their possible failure modes. This FMEA approach is sometimes used in product Design for Six Sigma (DFSS) projects.

- *The functional approach,* which recognizes that every item is designed to perform a number of functions that can be classified as outputs. The outputs are listed and their failure modes analyzed. This approach to FMEA is most common on both DMAIC and DMADV projects involving improvement of processes or complex systems.

FMEA Process

The FMEA is an integral part of early design process and it should take place during the Improve phase of DMAIC or the Design phase of DMADV. FMEAs are living documents and they must be updated to reflect design changes, which makes them useful in the Control or Verify phases as well. The analysis is used to assess high-risk items and the activities under way to provide corrective actions. The FMEA is also used to define special test considerations, quality inspection points, preventive maintenance actions, operational constraints, useful life, and other pertinent information and activities necessary to minimize failure risk. All recommended actions that result from the FMEA must be evaluated and formally dispositioned by appropriate implementation or documented rationale for no action. The following steps are used in performing an FMEA:

Define the system to be analyzed. Complete system definition includes identification of internal and interface functions, expected performance at all system levels, system restraints, and failure definitions. Functional narratives of the system should include

---

[1] Mil-Std-1629A actually calls the approach FMECA, which stands for Failure Mode, Effect, and Criticality Analysis, but over time the "C" has been dropped from common usage. However, criticality analysis is still very much a part of FMEA.

descriptions of each goal in terms of functions that identify tasks to be performed for each goal and operational mode. Narratives should describe the environmental profiles, expected cycle times and equipment utilization, and the functions and outputs of each item.

1. Construct process maps that illustrate the operation, interrelationships, and interdependencies of functional entities.

2. Conduct SIPOC (Supplier, Input, Process, Output, Customer) analysis for each subprocess in the system. All process and system interfaces should be indicated.

3. List the intended function of each step in the process or subprocess.

4. For each process step, identify all potential item and interface failure modes and define the effect on the immediate function or item, on the system, and on the mission to be performed for the customer.

5. Evaluate each failure mode in terms of the worst potential consequences that may result and assign a severity classification category (SEV). (See Table 6.)

6. Determine the likelihood of occurrence of each failure mode and assign an occurrence risk category (OCC). (See Table 6.)

7. Identify failure detection methods and assign a detectability risk category (DET). (See Table 6.)

8. Calculate the risk priority number (RPN) for the current system.

$$RPN = SEV \times OCC \times DET$$

9. Determine compensating provisions for each failure mode.

10. Identify corrective design or other actions required to eliminate failure or control the risk. Assign responsibility and due dates for corrective actions.

11. Identify effects of corrective actions on other system attributes.

12. Identify severity, occurrence, and detectability risks after the corrective action and calculate the "after" RPN.

13. Document the analysis and summarize the problems that could not be corrected and identify the special controls that are necessary to reduce failure risk.

Table 6. FMEA Severity, Likelihood, Detectability Rating Guidelines
Note: p is the estimated probability of failure **not** being detected.

Rating	Severity (SEV)	Occurrence (OCC)	Detectability (DET)
	How significant is this failure's effect to the customer?	How likely is the cause of this failure to occur?	How likely is it that the existing system will detect the cause, if the defect occurs?
1	Minor. Customer won't notice the effect or will consider it insignificant.	Not likely.	Nearly certain to detect before reaching the customer. (p ≈ 0)
2	Customer will notice the effect.	Documented low failure rate.	Extremely low probability of reaching the customer without detection. (0 < p > 0.01)
3	Customer will become irritated at reduced performance.	Undocumented low failure rate.	Low probability of reaching the customer without detection. (0.01 < p > 0.05)
4	Marginal. Customer dissatisfaction due to reduced performance.	Failures occur from time to time.	Likely to be detected before reaching the customer. (0.05 < p > 0.20)
5	Customer's productivity is reduced.	Documented moderate failure rate.	Might be detected before reaching the customer. (0.20 < p > 0.50)
6	Customer will complain. Repair or return likely. Increased internal costs (scrap, rework, etc.).	Undocumented moderate failure rate.	Unlikely to be detected before reaching the customer. (0.50 < p > 0.70)
7	Critical. Reduced customer loyalty. Internal operations adversely impacted.	Documented high failure rate.	Highly unlikely to detect before reaching the customer. (0.70 < p > 0.90)
8	Complete loss of customer goodwill. Internal operations disrupted.	Undocumented high failure rate.	Poor chance of detection. (0.90 < p > 0.95)
9	Customer or employee safety compromised. Regulatory compliance questionable.	Failures common.	Extremely poor chance of detection. (0.95 < p > 0.99)
10	Catastrophic. Customer or employee endangered without warning. Violation of law or regulation.	Failures nearly always occur.	Nearly certain that failure won't be detected. (p ≈ 1)

RPNs are useful in setting priorities, with higher RPNs receiving greater attention than lower RPNs. Some organizations have guidelines requiring action based on the absolute value of the RPN. For example, Boeing recommends that action be required if RPN > 120. Worksheet 41 can be used to document and guide the team in conducting an FMEA. Instructions for using Worksheet 41 are provided in Table 7. FMEA is incorporated into software packages, including some that perform QFD. There are numerous resources available on the Web to assist you with FMEA, including spreadsheets, real-world examples of FMEA, and much more.[2]

---

[2] www.fmeainfocentre.com.

Table 7. FMEA Information

General Information

- What is the product or process?
- Who prepared the FMEA?
- Who is on the Six Sigma team?
- What was the FMEA creation date?
- What is the date of the last revision?

Function	Potential Failure Mode	Potential Failure Effect	Potential Causes	Current Controls	Severity (SEV)	Occurrence (OCC)	Detection (DET)	RPN	Recommended Action	Responsibility and Due Date	Actions Taken	After SEV	After OCC	After DET	After RPN
Describe the process or product being analyzed. (A row number is often assigned.)	What could go wrong? What might the customer not like?	What happens to the customer if the failure occurs?	What might cause the failure to occur?	What systems are in place to prevent the cause or detect the failure?	A rating of 1 to 10 from Table 6	A rating of 1 to 10 from Table 6	A rating of 1 to 10 from Table 6	SEV * OCC * DET	What actions, if any, should be taken to reduce the RPN?	Who is responsible for the action? When is the action expected to be complete?	What was actually done to reduce the RPN?	A rating of 1 to 10 from Table	A rating of 1 to 10 from Table 6	A rating of 1 to 10 from Table 6	SEV * OCC * DET

Worksheet 41. FMEA Worksheet

General Information															
Function	Potential Failure Mode	Potential Failure Effect	Potential Causes	Current Controls	Severity (SEV)	Occurrence (OCC)	Detection (DET)	RPN	Recommended Action	Responsibility and Due Date	Actions Taken	After SEV	After OCC	After DET	After RPN

105

Issue#

Process Metrics

Six Sigma projects operate upon business processes. These processes are designed to deliver something of value to a customer, such as a product or a service. For this reason, these processes are sometimes called *customer value streams*. The purpose of most Six Sigma projects is to improve business processes so that they deliver greater value to customers. In this section you will determine precisely how the success of these efforts will be measured.

What Are the Key Metrics for This Business Process?

Six Sigma process metrics typically fall into one of three major categories: quality, cost, or schedule. These characteristics are critical to the success of the enterprise and are thus commonly referred to as "critical to" characteristics. A critical-to-quality characteristic (CTQ) is one that impacts on the fitness for use of the product or service produced by the process. A critical-to-cost (CTC) characteristic has a significant impact on the cost to produce the product or service. A critical-to-schedule (CTS) characteristic has a significant impact on the ability to deliver the product or service in a timely manner. Collectively, these are often called *CTx* characteristics, where x = Q for quality, C for cost, and S for schedule.

Note that it is often difficult to separate a metric into one and only one category. For example, if a Six Sigma project involved a coffee mug manufacturing process, a crack in a coffee mug would be classified as a CTQ characteristic even though cracked mugs also impact cost and schedule. Normally, the CTx is assigned to the dominant effect; in this case it is quality. An example of a CTC characteristic for the coffee mug process might be the energy consumed firing the ceramic. A CTS characteristic might be the timeliness of raw material deliveries.

DPMO Definition

Defects-per-million-opportunities (DPMO) criteria must be carefully defined. The *defect* must be described in clear, rigorous, and unambiguous terms. Defect definition often includes photos, physical specimens, or other inspection aids. Similar attention must be given to the *opportunity* used as the base. Opportunities are events or characteristics that might be incorrect.

Example: Wave solder. A defect would be an improperly produced solder joint. The defect might be missing solder, incomplete solder, poor solder bond, grainy solder, short circuits, etc. Each of these defects would be carefully defined and personnel would be thoroughly trained to identify each. A single solder joint might have several defects; all would be counted. The opportunities would be solder joints. DPMO would be calculated for this process as follows:

$$DPMO = 1,000,000 \frac{\text{defects}}{\text{number of solder joints}} \quad \text{(Equation 1)}$$

For example, for a circuit board with 1,000 solder joints and 5 defects, the DPMO would be:

$$DPMO = 1,000,000 \frac{5}{1,000} = 5,000 \quad \text{(Equation 2)}$$

The DPMO for a characteristic is measured as the process average DPMO.

Poorly chosen opportunity metrics can lead to "denominator management"—manipulation of the measurement system. For example, the opportunity metric for complete electronic units delivered to final assembly should be the number of units, not the number of solder joints in the units. A proper denominator reflects the process being measured, not an earlier process or subprocess. For example, if the process is creating solder joints, then solder joints are a proper opportunity measure. If the process is placing circuit boards into an electronics assembly, then we would count circuit boards, connectors, fasteners, etc. but not the constituent elements of these parts.

If you find that games are being played with the measurement system, list it as an issue to be resolved by the project sponsor, process owner, or management. If the issue is serious enough, consider classifying the project as "Stalled" until it is resolved. Six Sigma can't function in an environment where honest measurements are not available.

Worksheet 42. CTQ Characteristics

CTQ	Defect Definition	Opportunity Definition

Worksheet 43. CTS and CTC Characteristics

Characteristic	Type (CTS or CTC)	Description

Other Key Factors and Metrics

Not all important elements can be neatly quantified using the CTx approach, including some of the most important: e.g., employee morale, customer satisfaction, or the reaction of interested third parties in other areas or in the community. If these factors are not considered explicitly, they may be overlooked, perhaps leading to the failure of the project. In this section, list other factors that are important to the project's success and specify how you will ensure that they are dealt with properly.

Worksheet 44. Other Key Factors and Metrics

Key Factor	How Monitored and Assured

How Does This Project Move the Organization Toward Its Strategic Goals and Objectives?

You now have the information you need to estimate the contribution this project makes to the helping the organization reach its strategic goals and objectives. Use Worksheet 45 to describe the impact this project will have on key strategic goals.

Worksheet 45. Linkages to Enterprise Strategic Goals

Strategic Goal	Contribution from Project

111

Figure 19. Define Gate Criteria

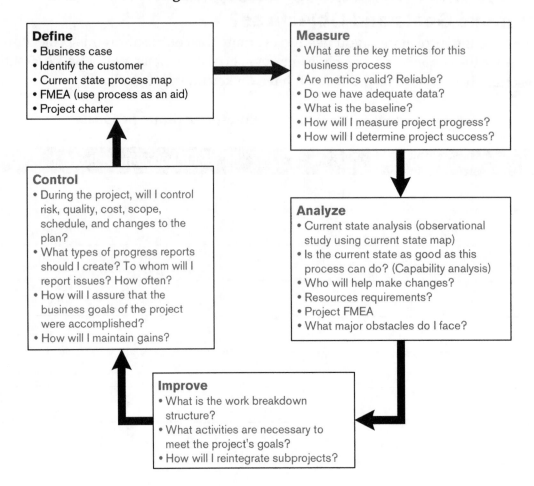

Define
- Business case
- Identify the customer
- Current state process map
- FMEA (use process as an aid)
- Project charter

Measure
- What are the key metrics for this business process
- Are metrics valid? Reliable?
- Do we have adequate data?
- What is the baseline?
- How will I measure project progress?
- How will I determine project success?

Control
- During the project, will I control risk, quality, cost, scope, schedule, and changes to the plan?
- What types of progress reports should I create? To whom will I report issues? How often?
- How will I assure that the business goals of the project were accomplished?
- How will I maintain gains?

Analyze
- Current state analysis (observational study using current state map)
- Is the current state as good as this process can do? (Capability analysis)
- Who will help make changes?
- Resources requirements?
- Project FMEA
- What major obstacles do I face?

Improve
- What is the work breakdown structure?
- What activities are necessary to meet the project's goals?
- How will I reintegrate subprojects?

Chapter 3
Measure

Measurement Reliability and Validity

Before trusting the information, it is important to verify that it is reliable and valid.

For our purposes, we will say that information is *reliable* if we obtain essentially the same information from more than one trusted source. For example, information on employee morale might be available from an employee focus group, employee interviews, and the annual employee survey.

We will say that information is *valid* if it covers the area of interest sufficiently well to accurately represent the area of interest. For example, if the process serves a seasonal market, the information should cover a complete business cycle, including the busy season and the slow season.

Dimensional Measurement Analysis

To evaluate the reliability and validity of dimensional measurement systems, such as gauges, conduct a *gauge repeatability and reproducibility* (R&R) study. Gauge R&R studies are scientifically designed to quantify gauge error from a variety of sources.

Worksheet 46. Gauge R&R Results

Gauge Description	ID #	Feature or Dimension	R&R Date	R&R Acceptable?	Issue #

Attribute Measurement Analysis[1]

Six Sigma projects usually involve metrics that are classifications rather than determinations of physical properties such as length, width, color, etc. The classifications can be *binary* (male/female, good/bad, failed/didn't fail, meets requirements/fails requirements, etc.), *nominal* (red-blue-green, shipped by truck/car/train, etc.), or *ordinal* (good-better-best, dissatisfied-satisfied-delighted). In this section, summarize the results of the measurement systems used to evaluate attributes data.

---

[1] Before completing this section of the *Planner*, study the background material in the section, "Attribute Measurement Error Analysis," starting on p. 216 in the Appendix.

Worksheet 47. Attribute Inspection System Results

Attribute	Operationally Defined?	Repeatability	Reproducibility	Accuracy	Bias	Issue #

Worksheet 48. Attribute Inspection Results by Inspector

Attribute	Inspector	Accurate?	Repeatable?	Unbiased	Stable?	Issue #

Figure 20. Measure Gate Criteria

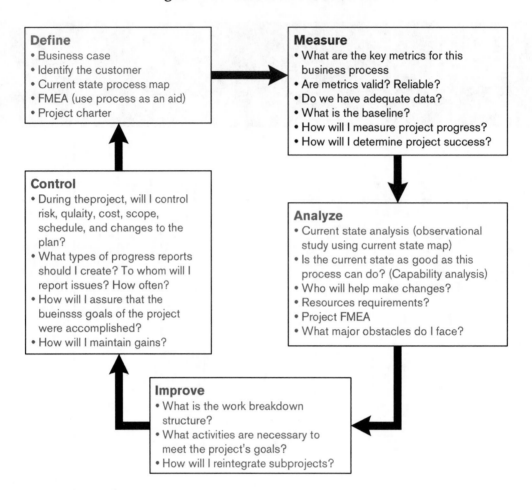

Define
- Business case
- Identify the customer
- Current state process map
- FMEA (use process as an aid)
- Project charter

Measure
- What are the key metrics for this business process
- Are metrics valid? Reliable?
- Do we have adequate data?
- What is the baseline?
- How will I measure project progress?
- How will I determine project success?

Control
- During theproject, will I control risk, qulaity, cost, scope, schedule, and changes to the plan?
- What types of progress reports should I create? To whom will I report issues? How often?
- How will I assure that the bueinsss goals of the project were accomplished?
- How will I maintain gains?

Analyze
- Current state analysis (observational study using current state map)
- Is the current state as good as this process can do? (Capability analysis)
- Who will help make changes?
- Resources requirements?
- Project FMEA
- What major obstacles do I face?

Improve
- What is the work breakdown structure?
- What activities are necessary to meet the project's goals?
- How will I reintegrate subprojects?

Chapter 4
Analyze

Analysis is the process of finding a solution to a problem. This involves two distinct steps:

1. Divergent thinking—to "cast a wide net" and include as many possible solution candidates as one can.

2. Convergent thinking—to identify the best solution.

In the *Analyze* phase of the Six Sigma project cycle, you must quantify the existing process to determine how best to achieve the process improvement goals. Tools and techniques useful during the analyze phase include:

- Run charts

- Descriptive statistical analysis (central tendency, spread, distribution, outliers)

- Exploratory data analysis (box plot comparisons, stem-and-leaf)

- SIPOC (Supplier, Input, Process, Output, Customer)

- Analytic data analysis (time series, SPC)

- Data mining: analysis of information contained in the enterprise data warehouse using automated or semi-automated means

- Process capability analysis

- Process yield analysis

- Scatter plots

- Correlation and regression analysis

- Categorical data analysis

- Nonparametric methods

Quantify the Current Process

Catalog of Data Sources for This Process

In executing Six Sigma projects, it is useful if everyone on the project team is aware of existing data on the process being improved. It is helpful if the team members spend some time compiling a list of these data sources, making knowledge of their existence available to everyone. Without an information catalog, team members often discover that they have wasted a great deal of time looking for or collecting information that other team members had at their fingertips.

Information can include knowledge of previous history of this process, data on past or current process performance, knowledge of suppliers and/or customers, knowledge of the informal leaders in the area, special technical expertise, etc. *Sources* can include persons with the knowledge, guardians of the data, names and contact information of the key players, Web addresses, book or report titles, file names, etc.

Worksheet 49. Information Resource Catalog

Information	Source

Exploratory Data Analysis

Exploratory data analysis (EDA) is conducted to collect evidence that will form the basis of theories of cause and effect. Are there gaps in the data? Are there patterns that suggest some mechanism at work? Do outliers occur?

Figure 21. Some EDA Techniques[1]

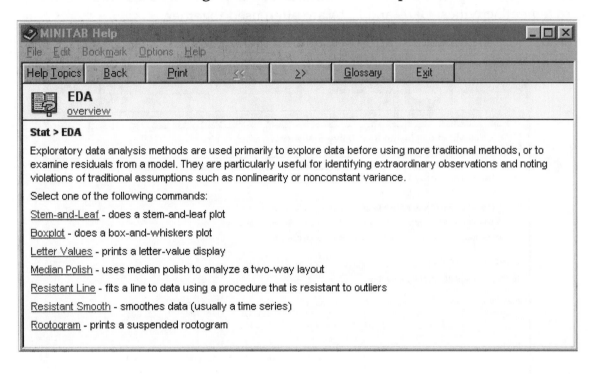

---

[1] Portions of MINITAB Statistical Software input and output contained in this book are printed with permission of Minitab Inc.

Descriptive Data Analysis

Descriptive data analysis (DDA) is conducted to determine what sort of distributions processes produce. Statistics are computed and graphical displays are created to explore the central tendency, spread, shape, outlier patterns, etc. This information is used to help form theories of cause and effect that can then be examined more carefully with SPC or designed experiments. The results are used to plan fact-based future process improvement activities. DDA and EDA are often used together.

Figure 22. Example of Combined DDA and EDA Analysis[2]

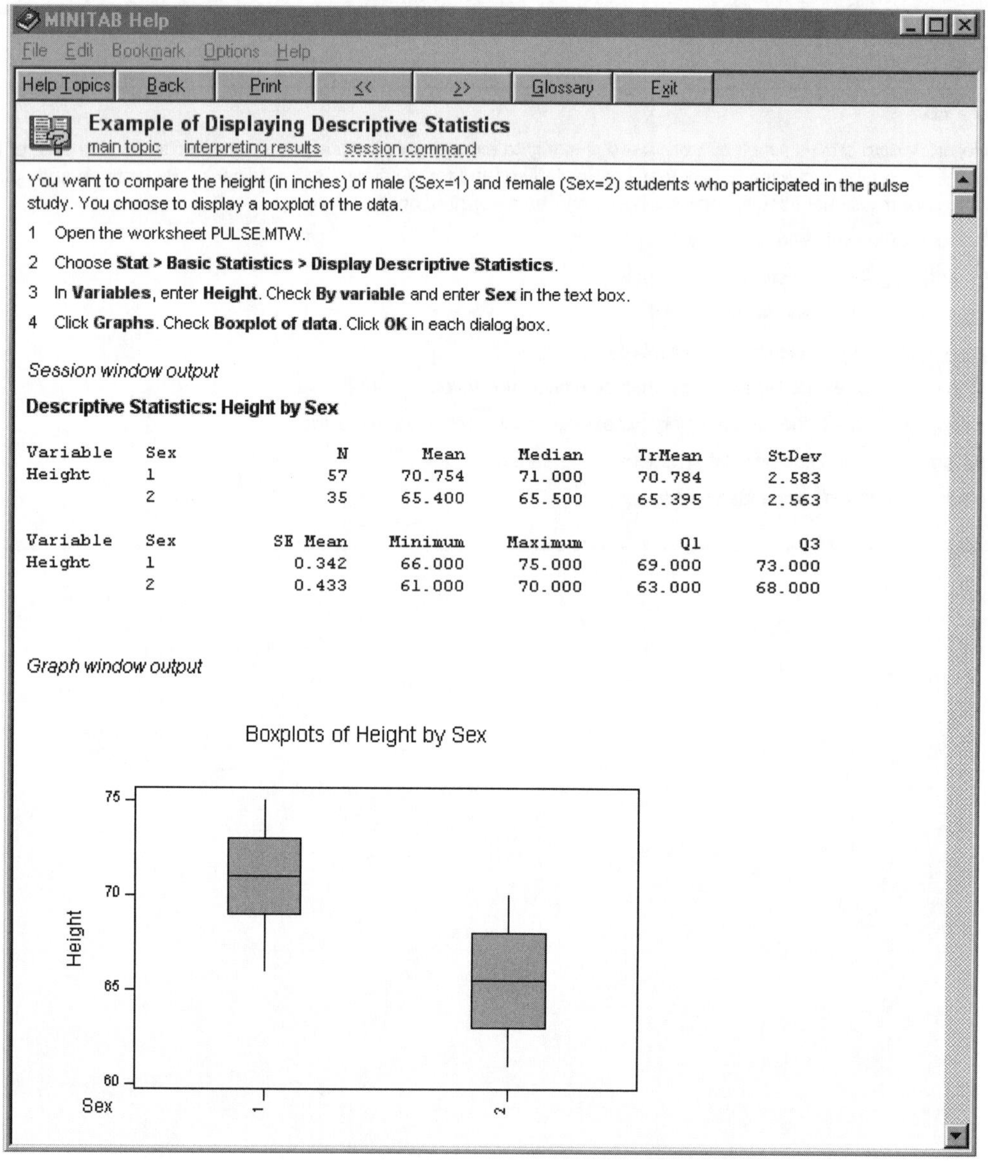

```
MINITAB Help                                                    _ □ ×
File  Edit  Bookmark  Options  Help
┌──────────┬───────┬───────┬──────┬──────┬─────────┬──────┐
│Help Topics│ Back │ Print │  <<  │  >>  │ Glossary │ Exit │
└──────────┴───────┴───────┴──────┴──────┴─────────┴──────┘
```

Example of Displaying Descriptive Statistics
main topic   interpreting results   session command

You want to compare the height (in inches) of male (Sex=1) and female (Sex=2) students who participated in the pulse study. You choose to display a boxplot of the data.

1   Open the worksheet PULSE.MTW.

2   Choose **Stat > Basic Statistics > Display Descriptive Statistics**.

3   In **Variables**, enter **Height**. Check **By variable** and enter **Sex** in the text box.

4   Click **Graphs**. Check **Boxplot of data**. Click **OK** in each dialog box.

Session window output

Descriptive Statistics: Height by Sex

Variable	Sex	N	Mean	Median	TrMean	StDev
Height	1	57	70.754	71.000	70.784	2.583
	2	35	65.400	65.500	65.395	2.563

Variable	Sex	SE Mean	Minimum	Maximum	Q1	Q3
Height	1	0.342	66.000	75.000	69.000	73.000
	2	0.433	61.000	70.000	63.000	68.000

Graph window output

Boxplots of Height by Sex

---

[2] Portions of MINITAB Statistical Software input and output contained in this book are printed with permission of Minitab Inc.

Worksheet 50. DDA/EDA-Based Theories to Investigate Further

Data-Based Observation	Hypothesized Cause	Hypothesis Investigation	Result, Cross-Reference

Example of Using Worksheet

Refer to the output shown in Figure 22. Now, it would seem a simple matter to conclude that females are shorter than males. And this certainly squares with our perception of the world, making it even easier to jump to that particular conclusion. Indeed, this is the sort of thing that is usually done in the business world. We have a preconceived notion, collect some data that "confirm" our notion, and conclude:

1. We were right all along.

2. The data collection exercise was a waste of time.

3. We can continue "hip-shooting" our way to success.

The problem is that this retrospective approach to data analysis is inadequate as a way to confirm hypotheses. Its purpose is to help us *develop* hypotheses. Here are only a few reasons why we can't conclude that the data in Figure 22 support the conclusion without further analysis:

- Maybe the males and females were children of different ages.

- Maybe the males and females we're interested in as customers are from different populations than used in the "happenstance" sample.

- Maybe the males were of one racial or ethnic group and the females were of another.

- Maybe the males and females we're interested in as customers are from different racial or ethnic groups.

The list could go on and on. The point is, to *confirm* the hypotheses suggested by the data, we must conduct another study in which we exercise a degree of control over the sampling and/or the experiment.

Figure 23 gives an example of how to document these sorts of results.

Figure 23. Example of Evaluating a Hypothesis

Data-Based Observation	Hypothesized Cause	Hypothesis Investigation	Result
Males appear to be taller than females. The data were obtained from a public database.	Natural difference between the sexes.	Our toys are marketed to American boys and girls aged 9 to 12. We will randomly sample 200 children in each year of our target market age groups (ages 9, 10, 11, and 12) and determine their heights.	Our samples show that there is a statistically significant difference on average, but the difference is much smaller than the original data indicated and varies by age. See "Age Ht study.htm" for details.

Quantify the Capability of the Current Process

Six Sigma is a data-driven approach to business process improvement. Data often indicate that the *capability* of the existing process far exceeds its *actual* performance level. In some cases the process can be dramatically improved at little or no cost. It is not uncommon to find that, once it is optimized, the process can meet the project goal.

Conduct a Process Audit

Before preparing a project plan, the Six Sigma project team should perform a detailed, physical audit of the process. One way to accomplish this is to form a process audit team. Six Sigma project team members who have in-depth knowledge of the proper way to operate the process should be members of the team, of course. However, it is also helpful to have team members who are less familiar with the project on the team. These "non-experts" often ask the 'dumb questions' that lead to true breakthrough thinking. The audit check sheet shown on the following pages can be used for simple process audits. The audit team should add additional items as required.

Process owners should be notified in advance of the audit, they should be kept informed during the audit, and they should be the first to receive the audit findings. We are interested in improving processes, not assigning blame. It may be helpful to have the project sponsor arrange the audit.

Worksheet 51. Process Audit Check Sheet

Process Description	
Process Owner	
Audit Team Members	
Audit Date(s)	

Item	Findings	Responsibility	Due Date	Issue #
Has the proper operation of this process been documented?				
Are personnel properly trained?				
Is this process being operated properly?				
Is the process operated consistently by various people?				
Have key process metrics been defined?				
Are they measured in a timely fashion?				

Item	Findings	Responsibility	Due Date	Issue #
Is the information easily available to those who need it?				
Is the process operated differently at different times of the week, month, or year?				
Are there simple things that can be done right away to improve this process? (e.g., lean manufacturing, main-tenancy, rearranging the workplace)				
Can poka-yoke (foolproofing) be applied to eliminate the *effects* of human errors without additional inspection?				
Would a simple procedure or policy change lead to dramatic improvement?				

Item	Findings	Responsibility	Due Date	Issue #

Prepare an Audit Report

After receiving the response from the process owner, the audit team should prepare a written audit report. The audit report should document the findings of the audit team, including recommendations for remedial action, actions already taken or planned by the process owner, the names of persons responsible for the action items, and deadlines for completing each action items.

The audit follow-up plan can be considered a subproject. The report should first be presented to the process owner and then revised if necessary. The final report should be presented to the entire Six Sigma project team for approval. Upon approval by the team, a summary report should be sent to the project sponsor. The Summary Audit Report, or its location, should be included in the Appendix of the *Planner* in the Audit Report section on p. 207.

Determine Sigma and DPMO Levels for CTx's

Critical-to-quality characteristics are measured in terms of defects per million opportunities. CTQs and DPMO *criteria* were established previously, in the Define phase (p. 106). We will now analyze these metrics.

At this point in the Six Sigma project, data are collected and the exact quality levels determined for all CTQ characteristics and for many CTC and CTS characteristics. This information will help us with our move forward planning by telling us if the existing business process has the *potential* to deliver quality levels that meet our project goals. It also tells us what the process is *actually* delivering. By comparing these two values, we can measure the *actual-potential gap*. Actual and potential performance must also be compared with the best practices performance levels determined in the future state description (p. 144).

Process Capability and Process Actual Sigma Levels for Continuous CTx Characteristics

For CTx's measured on a continuous scale, we will use calculated sigma levels to measure process performance, e.g., a sigma level of 6 would indicate 3.4 PPM performance. We call data obtained for CTx's measured on a continuous scale *variables data*.

Measuring Process Capability for Variables Data[3]

Imagine a process operated in a state of perfect statistical control. For a variable CTx, this state is operationalized when the X-bar and range or sigma charts indicate no special causes for an extended period of time. In Six Sigma analysis, when this stable state exists, the process capability is measured by using the process mean and standard deviation and assuming a 1.5σ shift will take place in the long term. Process reject rates

---

[3] Note: Although capability indices (Cpk, etc.) are equivalent to Z-scores, we will not discuss process capability indices here. For more information on relating Z statistics to these indices, see *The Six Sigma Handbook*, Chapter 13.

are found for the lower and upper specifications using normal tables or software. Finally, the combined process reject rate is used to determine the process RTY and sigma level.

Perfect statistical control is not common. In practice, if control charts are in statistical control for 90% of the time or more, then the process capability is approximated by dropping the out-of-control groups from the calculations. However, this mathematical trick should not be used unless the root causes of the out-of-control conditions have been identified.

Example

The CTQ for a machining process is the diameter of a pin. The specifications call for the diameter to be 1.000 ± 0.001 inches. A control chart shows statistical control for an entire workweek. The average of the X-bar chart is 1.0001 inches and, based on the sigma chart, the standard deviation is 0.0002 inches. What is the process capability sigma level?

Solution

$$Z_{\text{Low Spec}} = \frac{\bar{X} - \text{Low Spec.}}{\sigma} = \frac{1.0001 - 0.9990}{0.0002} = 5.5$$

$$DPMO = 13.7$$

$$Z_{\text{High Spec}} = \frac{\text{High Spec.} - \bar{X}}{\sigma} = \frac{1.0010 - 1.0001}{0.0002} = 4.5$$

$$DPMO = 1350$$

Process DPMO = 1363.7

Process sigma level = 4.5

Measuring Actual Process Performance for Variables Data

Assume that the process does *not* show statistical control. Or assume that we must measure a CTx dimension without knowledge of the production sequence. This state describes the *actual process performance*. When this situation exists, then the process performance is measured by using the sample mean and standard deviation and assuming a 1.5σ shift. The calculations are identical to those above, except that now the sample standard deviation is not obtained from a range or sigma chart showing statistical control, i.e., it is not computed from rational subgroups. Instead sigma is computed from aggregated data, for example, using a calculator or spreadsheet formula on the entire data set.

Example

Assume the same process as in the previous example. The CTQ for a machining process is the diameter of a pin. As before, the specifications call for the diameter to be $1.000 \pm$

0.001 inches. However, instead of using rational subgroups from a control chart, a random sample of 50 items is measured and the average and standard deviation are computed. The average is 1.0001 inches and the standard deviation is 0.0004 inches. What is the process actual sigma level?

Solution

$$Z_{\text{Low Spec}} = \frac{\bar{X} - \text{Low Spec.}}{s} = \frac{1.0001 - 0.9990}{0.0004} = 2.75$$

$$DPMO = 105,649.8$$

$$Z_{\text{High Spec}} = \frac{\text{High Spec.} - \bar{X}}{s} = \frac{1.0010 - 1.0001}{0.0004} = 2.25$$

$$DPMO = 226,627.3$$

Process Actual DPMO = 332,277.1

Process actual sigma level = 1.93

Note: The sigma level of 1.93 represents *actual* process performance, not capability. The difference of 330,913.4 PPM (the DPMO based on a random sample vs. the DPMO based on rational subgroups from a stable process) is the actual-potential gap. A large gap suggests that process improvement should focus on finding and eliminating special causes of variation, i.e., focusing on the variability of performance. A small gap would indicate that the team should focus on process redesign, i.e., focusing on the average level of performance.

Process Capability and Process Actual Sigma Levels for Attribute CTx Characteristics

Many CTx characteristics are not measured in terms of physical properties like weight, size, etc. Instead, occurrences are counted. Examples include:

- customer complaints
- warranty claims
- number of product returns
- product defects
- errors in data entry
- programming errors
- errors on engineering drawings
- missed delivery deadlines
- customer defections to competitors
- customers who give the company the highest rating in a survey
- units scrapped or reworked

The list is endless. In Six Sigma, data on these characteristics are called *attribute data* or *discrete data*. Process capability and actual process and product performance must also be determined for attribute characteristics. While the basic procedure is the same as that used to determine process capability sigma level and actual performance for variables, the calculations themselves are different.

Measuring Process Capability for Attributes Data

For an attribute CTx, a state of perfect statistical control is operationalized when the appropriate control charts (usually c, p, np, or U charts)[4] indicate no special causes for an extended period of time. This state describes the *process capability* for the attribute. When this state exists, then the process capability is measured by using the process mean for the attribute, assuming a 1.5σ shift. Since the control chart measures the attribute directly, there is no need for table lookups to determine the DPMO levels.

As with CTx measures of variables data, complete statistical control is not common for attribute data. If control charts are in statistical control for, say, 90% of the time, then the process capability is usually approximated by dropping the out-of-control groups from the calculations. However, this mathematical trick should not be done unless the causes of the out-of-control conditions have been identified. *This is especially important for attribute data, because it may be that the special cause of better-than-normal performance provides clues for process improvement.*

Example

A company is concerned about the error rate of a particular type of billing statement it sends to customers. A control chart of weekly errors per 1,000 bills indicates statistical control for two quarters (26 weeks). The average of the control chart (a c-chart) is 7.5 errors per 1,000 bills. What are the process capability (DPMO) and sigma level?

Solution

Once statistical control has been achieved, the process average can be used to estimate the DPMO level. The average of 7.5 errors per 1000 bills is equivalent to a DPMO level of 7,500. Adjusting for the 1.5σ shift gives a process sigma level of 3.9.

Measuring Actual Process Performance for Variables Data

If the process does not show statistical control or if we must measure a CTx attribute without knowledge of the production sequence, then we cannot determine the process capability. However, we can still describe *actual* process performance for the attribute. Actual process DPMO performance is measured by using the sample mean. Product or process sigma levels are calculated assuming a 1.5σ shift. The calculations are identical to those above, except the sample mean is not obtained from a control chart in statistical control. I.e., it is not computed from subgroups in a time-ordered sequence.

---

[4] *Six Sigma Handbook,* Chapter 12.

Example

Assume the same process as in the previous example, i.e., the error rate for a billing process. However, we do not know the production sequence of the bills. All we know is that during the previous 26 weeks 10 million bills were sent and 75,000 errors were identified by customers. What is the process actual DPMO and sigma level?

Solution

The aggregate data can be used to estimate the actual DPMO level, but not the process capability. The reported error rate is equivalent to a DPMO level of 7,500. Adjusting for the 1.5σ shift gives a process sigma level of 3.9.

Note: The sigma level of 3.9 represents *actual* process performance, not capability. Without the information contained in the time sequence, it is not possible to determine capability. Remember: when the goal is to understand a dynamic business process, knowledge of the production sequence of the data is vital.

Worksheet 52. Actual CTx DPMO and Sigma Levels

Characteristic	Actual DPMO	$\dfrac{DPMO}{1,000,000}$	Yield $= 1 - \dfrac{DPMO}{1,000,000}$	Sigma Level

Worksheet 53. Capability Levels of Performance[5]

Characteristic	Capability DPMO	$\dfrac{DPMO}{1,000,000}$	Yield = $1 - \dfrac{DPMO}{1,000,000}$	Sigma Level

---

[5] Calculate sigma using rational subgroups from a stable process.

Worksheet 54. Rolled Throughput Yield Analysis

RTY Capability (potential)	
RTY Actual	
Actual-Potential Gap	
Project RTY Goal	

Things to consider:

- How large are the gaps among the actual RTY, the capability RTY, and the project's goal RTY?

- Does actual process performance indicate a need for a breakthrough project?

- Would we need a breakthrough project if we operated up to capability?

- The RTY cannot be better than the lowest yield for all product features or process steps. Use this fact to help allocate project resources. For example, would applying SPC to a subset of CTx's achieve the project's goals at lower cost?

Notes:

Figure 24. Analyze Gate Criteria

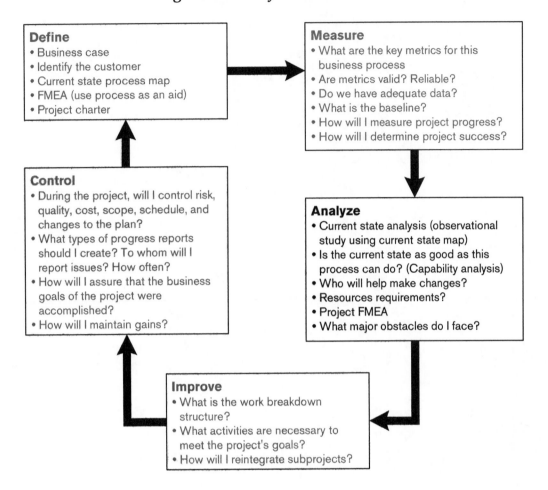

Define
- Business case
- Identify the customer
- Current state process map
- FMEA (use process as an aid)
- Project charter

Measure
- What are the key metrics for this business process
- Are metrics valid? Reliable?
- Do we have adequate data?
- What is the baseline?
- How will I measure project progress?
- How will I determine project success?

Control
- During the project, will I control risk, quality, cost, scope, schedule, and changes to the plan?
- What types of progress reports should I create? To whom will I report issues? How often?
- How will I assure that the business goals of the project were accomplished?
- How will I maintain gains?

Analyze
- Current state analysis (observational study using current state map)
- Is the current state as good as this process can do? (Capability analysis)
- Who will help make changes?
- Resources requirements?
- Project FMEA
- What major obstacles do I face?

Improve
- What is the work breakdown structure?
- What activities are necessary to meet the project's goals?
- How will I reintegrate subprojects?

Chapter 5
Improve

To some extent, the Analyze and Improve phases are conducted simultaneously. In fact, there is Improvement in every phase of the project. The work done in the Define, Measure, and Analyze phases all help better determine what the customer wants, how to measure it, and what the existing process can do to provide it. It is possible that, by the time the Improve phase has been reached, so much improvement will have already been made that the project goals have been met. If so, the project may be concluded. However, if the process performance still falls short of the project's goals, then additional activities in the improvement phase must be undertaken.

Important Note

In the Six Sigma DMAIC cycle, "Improve" precedes "Control." While this is true for process improvement, there is an exception to this sequential approach when it comes to project *management*. The exception is for *project control planning*. Management of improvement projects cannot be separated from project control. The following project control plans should be completed as soon as the required information is available:

- Risk control plan (p. 72)

- Quality plan (p. 80)

- Cost control plan (p. 84)

- Schedule control plan (p. 87)

- Project change control plan (p. 208)

To accomplish this, the team will need to move back and forth between the Improve and Control sections. To begin, complete as much as possible of each control plan before beginning the Improve phase. Add additional detail to the various control plans as more information becomes available. For example, complete the schedule control plan when the project schedule has been completed.

Optimize the Process

There is still one last chance to conclude the project without an extensive process or product redesign: optimization. Optimization involves a rigorous, detailed study of the existing process to determine if there is any way to operate it such that the requirements are met at levels near six sigma.

Statistical Design of Experiments (DOE) can help determine the optimal performance levels in terms of the various CTx's. It is important that, before we experiment with a process, we first determine its capability if it is operated consistently in accordance with established procedures, as we did in the Analyze phase. There are many reasons for first determining the process capability:

- Experiments may not be necessary if procedures are rigorously followed, thus eliminating the need for process optimization experiments.

- Experiments are costly.

- Experiments disrupt operations.

- Experiments are inherently risky and may lead to additional problems.

- Experiments may produce misleading results if process variation isn't reduced beforehand.

- Variables to experiment on are often discovered while auditing a process, performing capability studies, or investigating special causes.

- Levels at which to set (or not set) experimental variables may be determined during the initial process investigation.

- Key personnel may be identified during auditing or SPC, thus helping us design a better experiment.

- "Noise" variables that need to be monitored during experiments may be identified during SPC investigations.

- The scope of the experiment is easier to determine if the process is well understood. By definition, we don't understand an unstable process as well as one we can control.

At this point in the project, we know the actual performance of the critical characteristics for this process and what the process is capable of doing if it is operated according to established procedures. However, it is possible that the process can do much better if we *changed* established procedures.

It is common practice, when new products or processes are introduced, to start out with very poor yields, often in the single-digit range. Process designers work diligently to improve things until they are called away by more urgent matters. At that point things are "carved in stone," i.e., the process is documented in standard operating procedure manuals and further changes to it are forbidden unless special permission is obtained. Although the standardized process may be much better than when it was introduced as a pilot, there is often a great deal of room for additional improvement. This is especially true if the SOP was written in the pre-Six Sigma era, when failures were still measured in percentages (parts per hundred) rather than DPMO (parts per million).

How much better might a process do? Listen to this true story.

A major computer manufacturer sold a wave solder machine because it believed that the best solder joints the machine could do were about 5 defects per thousand (DPMO = 5,000 or a yield of 99.9%). Its new wave solder machine was 10 times better, i.e., the defect rate improved to 500 PPM. Naturally, the company felt its investment was worthwhile. Some years later, it acquired the company that had purchased the old solder equipment. To their amazement, the old solder machine was 100 times better than the new one! The defect rate was only 5 PPM, or nearly six sigma.

The lesson here is that we should do all that we can to optimize the existing process before spending large sums of money for new technology. At this point in the project, the Black Belt should review the data gathered previously to determine if DOE is indicated. If so, the Black Belt should assemble the necessary personnel and conduct DOEs to determine the optimal levels at which the process can be operated. DOE results can be summarized in the tables on this and the following pages.

Perform Designed Experiments

At this time, conduct designed experiments to determine the optimum settings for the process. Optimum settings are those that maximize the process yield, both overall and for each CTx. Process optimization is generally conducted in five phases, as shown in Table 8.[1] At the completion of each phase, the team should compare the process performance with the project's goals. If the process is stable at a level that meets the project's goals, determine if the project should continue or if another project should be pursued instead.

Table 8. Phases in Process Optimization

Phase	Description	Purpose
0	Getting your bearings	Conducted using data mining, DDA, EDA, and SPC to determine how the process behaved historically, how it is behaving now, and what can be done to stabilize it.
1	Screening experiment	Determine which of many possible variables is having an effect on the result.
2	Steepest ascent	After identifying important main effects, a fractional factorial experiment is conducted to determine the amount to change each important variable to move most quickly toward the optimum. A simple, linear model is assumed. Changes are made incrementally until performance peaks.
3	Factorial experiment	Factorial experiments are conducted near the settings where performance peaked to identify variable effects and interactions in greater detail. Multivariable interactions are investigated. Center points are added to the model to allow estimation of curvature.
4	Response surface design	Composite design experiments are conducted to map the region near the optimum. The goal is to find settings for the variables where the results are consistently close to the optimum.

After completing the process optimization phases, summarize the results using Worksheet 55 and Worksheet 56.

---

[1] *Six Sigma Handbook*, Chapter 17.

Worksheet 55. Optimum Levels of Performance[2]

Characteristic	Optimum DPMO	Optimum Yield =	Sigma Level

---

[2] Determined by conducting statistically designed experiments.

Worksheet 56. Optimum Rolled Throughput Yields

RTY Optimum	
RTY Actual	
Actual-Optimum Gap	
Project RTY Goal	

Things to consider:
- How large are the gaps among the optimum RTY, the actual RTY, and the project's goal RTY?

- Would we need a breakthrough project if the process operated at optimum?

- The RTY cannot be better than the lowest yield for all product features or process steps. Use this fact to help allocate project resources. For example, would optimizing a subset of CTx's achieve the project's goals at lower cost?

Notes:

What Will the Future State Be?

The future state is the reality that will be created when the project is successfully completed. It is a vision of the future. In this new future, progress will have been made. In this section, the team will define the future state in explicit terms. Doing so will provide the project team and the sponsor with a common vision of their destination.

What Are the Best Practices in This Area?

Before setting goals for the future state, it is helpful to know what the best-in-class performance is for similar processes. The study of best-in-class process performance is known as *benchmarking*. Benchmarking involves research into the best practices at the industry, firm, or process level.

Benchmarking goes beyond identifying "industry standards." A standard isn't a best practice; it's a *standard* practice. There is no competitive advantage gained from standard performance. Benchmarking breaks the firm's activities down to process operations and looks for the best-in-class for a particular operation. Black Belts should conduct research as follows:

Worksheet 57. Benchmarking Step 1: Identify What Is to Be Benchmarked

Express the activity in generic terms—e.g., delivering packages, handling highly erratic workloads, storing dangerous materials, moving delicate equipment, order fulfillment.

Worksheet 58. Benchmarking Step 2: Identify Comparative Companies

Consult books, trade magazines, industry award announcements, quality award recipients, the Internet, your firm's supplier database, etc. to identify those organizations that excel at the process or activity. You may also want to ask field personnel, consultants, suppliers, sales personnel, and customers for opinions on who is the best in a particular area.

Worksheet 59. Benchmarking Step 3: Determine Data Collection Methods

Determine what data are relevant and plan a search strategy. Data collection methods might include industry databases, newspapers, asking the benchmark firm for data, SEC reports or other public documents, etc. Consider site visits.

Worksheet 60. Benchmarking Step 4: Collect Data on Benchmark

Quantify the benchmark operation using metrics that can be compared with your internal metrics.

Worksheet 61. Benchmarking Step 5: Determine the Current Performance Gap

What is the magnitude of the difference between current performance and benchmark performance?

Worksheet 62. Benchmarking Step 6: Identify Causes of the Performance Gap

What is done differently at the benchmark process? Create a catalog of these differences.

Worksheet 63. Benchmarking Step 7: Estimate Future Performance Levels

Determine how benchmark metrics will be applied in your project.

Worksheet 64. Benchmarking Step 8: Establish Functional Goals and Gain Acceptance of Stakeholders

Create timetables for improving your performance.

Create a Future State Process Map

Use the benchmarking findings to develop the design for new process. Using the icons shown in **Error! Reference source not found.**Worksheet 65, draw process maps describing possible future states of the business process. How does the future process deliver value to the customer? What is the flow of the process? Use additional pages if necessary.

Figure 25. Example of a Future State Process Map

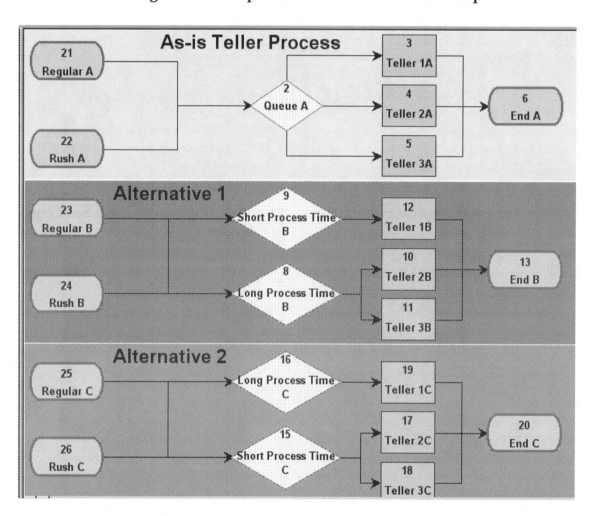

Worksheet 65. Alternative Future State Process Maps

How Will the Future State Be Better than the Current State?

Compare the future process with the current process.

Worksheet 66. Future State Improvement Estimates

Undesirable Effect or CTx	Current Process	Est. Future Process

151

Six Sigma Project Activities Template

At this stage it is time to pursue breakthrough improvement by doing the activities in a Six Sigma plan. Although every project is unique, most Six Sigma projects that use the DMAIC framework have many tasks in common, at least at a general level. Many people find it helpful if to have a generic template to use for planning their project activities. This is especially true when the Black Belt or Green Belt is new and has limited project management experience. Table 9 can be used as a tool by Six Sigma teams. It shows typical tasks and responsibilities for each major phase of a typical Six Sigma project.

Table 9. Typical DMAIC Project Tasks and Responsibilities

Task	Responsibility
Plan Project	
• Identify opportunity for improvement	Leadership
• Identify sponsor	Leadership
• Select team members	Sponsor, Black Belt
• Complete project charter	Black Belt
• Estimate savings	Black Belt
• Draft project charter	Black Belt, Sponsor
• Review/accept project charter	Sponsor, Process Owner
Define	
• Team training	Black Belt, Green Belt
• Review existing process documentation	Team Member, Process Expert
• Define project objectives and plan	Team
• Present objectives and plan to management	Green Belt
• Define and map as-is process	Team, Process Expert
• Review and redefine problem, if necessary	Team
• Sponsor review	
Measure	
• Identify CTQs	Green Belt, Black Belt
• Collect data on subtasks and cycle time	Team
• Validate measurement system	Black Belt, Process Operator

Task	Responsibility
Analyze	
• Prepare baseline graphs on subtasks/cycle time	Black Belt, Green Belt
• Analyze impacts, e.g., subtasks, ANOM (Analysis of Means), Pareto …	Black Belt, Green Belt
• Use subteams to analyze time and value, risk management	Black Belt, Green Belt
• Benchmark other companies	Team Member
• Discuss subteams' preliminary findings	Team
• Consolidate subteams' analyses/findings	Team
Improve	
• Present recommendations to process owners and operators	Sponsor, Team
• Review recommendations/formulate pilot	Team, Black Belt
• Prepare for improved process pilot	Team, Process Owner
• Test improved process (run pilot)	Process Operator
• Analyze pilot and results	Black Belt, Green Belt
• Develop implementation plan	Team, Process Owner
• Prepare final presentation	Team
• Present final recommendations to management team	Green Belt
Control	
• Define control metrics	Black Belt, Green Belt, Process Expert
• Develop metrics collection tool	Black Belt
• Roll out improved process	Process Owner
• Roll out control metrics	Process Owner
• Monitor process monthly using control metrics	Process Owner, Black Belt

The detailed project plan was completed previously in the Planning phase. The boilerplate presented in Table 9 should be used only to provide high-level guidance.

Presentation and Acceptance of Deliverables

The *Improve* phase concludes when the project deliverables are accepted by the project sponsor. Successful project completion is *the* major milestone of the project; it should be viewed as a "big deal" and treated accordingly. Formal presentation of the project deliverables to the sponsor is recommended; project team members should be recognized for their contribution. The acceptance should be official. Project sponsors and other "customers" who receive the deliverables should indicate their acceptance with a signature.

The customers for project deliverables were specified in the section entitled "Develop the Project Charter" (p. 1). Deliverables were described in the section entitled "How Will I Measure Project Success?" (p. 18). Also see the section "How Will the Future State Be Better than the Current State?" (p. 151). This information should now be reviewed and used to summarize the results of the project using Worksheet 67. Deliverables Acceptance Report.

Worksheet 67. Deliverables Acceptance Report[*]

Deliverable Promised	Delivered	Date	Sponsor or Customer Acceptance

---

[*] Part of the official project plan.

Figure 26. Improve Gate Criteria

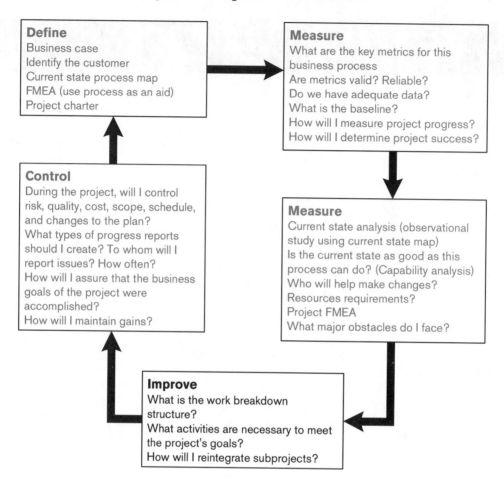

Define
Business case
Identify the customer
Current state process map
FMEA (use process as an aid)
Project charter

Measure
What are the key metrics for this
business process
Are metrics valid? Reliable?
Do we have adequate data?
What is the baseline?
How will I measure project progress?
How will I determine project success?

Control
During the project, will I control
risk, quality, cost, scope, schedule,
and changes to the plan?
What types of progress reports
should I create? To whom will I
report issues? How often?
How will I assure that the business
goals of the project were
accomplished?
How will I maintain gains?

Measure
Current state analysis (observational
study using current state map)
Is the current state as good as this
process can do? (Capability analysis)
Who will help make changes?
Resources requirements?
Project FMEA
What major obstacles do I face?

Improve
What is the work breakdown
structure?
What activities are necessary to meet
the project's goals?
How will I reintegrate subprojects?

Chapter 6
Control

The scientific principle of *entropy* states that, left to themselves, things tend to move from an orderly state to a more disorderly state. This is certainly true for project plans and for business systems. Unless we pay attention to the plans we've developed so carefully and institutionalize the process improvements we worked so hard to accomplish, entropy will set in and things will deteriorate. In this section of the Six Sigma Project Planner we will develop controls to ensure that we keep our hard-won gains. This is the "C" in the Six Sigma DMAIC performance improvement cycle.

Control Failure Mode and Effect Analysis (FMEA)

FMEA was used earlier, in the Define phase, to identify problems with the current process or product (p. 100). It is now conducted to help develop control plans that *prevent* problems with the new process. The procedure is the same as used in the earlier analysis, only now you will consider the new process or product.

Worksheet 68. Control FMEA Worksheet

General Information

Function	Potential Failure Mode	Potential Failure Effect	Potential Causes	Current Controls	Severity (SEV)	Occurrence (OCC)	Detection (DET)	RPN	Recommended Action	Responsibility and Due Date	Actions Taken	"After" SEV	"After" OCC	"After" DET	"After" RPN

158

Business Process Control Systems

You've met the project's goals and the customer and sponsor have accepted the deliverables. The project has finished successfully! Or has it? Don't be too quick to declare victory. The last battle is yet to be fought—the battle against creeping disorder, the battle against entropy, the battle to ensure that the gains are permanent.

How Will We Maintain the Gains Made?

All organizations have systems designed to ensure stability and to protect against undesirable change. Often these systems also make it more difficult to make beneficial change; perhaps you encountered an example or two while pursuing your Six Sigma project! Still, once you've created an improved business system, these "anti-change" systems can be your friend. Here are some suggestions of ways to protect your hard-won gains.

- *Policy changes*. Which corporate policies should be changed as a result of the project? Have some policies been rendered obsolete? Are new policies needed?

- *New standards*. Did the project bring the organization into compliance with a standard (e.g., ISO 9000, environmental standards, product safety standards)? If so, adopting the standard might prevent backsliding. Are there any industry standards that, if adopted, would help maintain the benefits of the project? Customer standards? Standards from ANSI, SAE, JCAHO, NCQA, ASTM, ASQ, or other standard-making organization? Government standards?

- *Modify procedures*. Procedures describe the way things are supposed to be done. Since the project produced better (different) results, presumably some things are being done differently. Be sure these differences are incorporated into formal procedures.

- *Modify quality appraisal and audit criteria*. The quality control activity in an organization exists to ensure conformance to requirements. This will work for you by ensuring that the changes made to documentation will result in changes in the way the work is done.

- *Update contract bid models*. The way product is priced for sale is directly related to profit, loss, and business success. Because of this, project improvements that are embedded in bid models and price models will be institutionalized by being indirectly integrated into an array of accounting and information systems.

- *Change engineering drawings*. Many Six Sigma projects create engineering change requests as part of their problem solution. For example, when a Six Sigma project evaluates process capability, it is common to discover that the engineering requirements are excessively tight. Perhaps designers used worst-case tolerancing instead of statistical tolerancing. The project team should ensure that these discoveries result in changes to engineering drawings.

- *Change manufacturing planning.* An organization's manufacturing plans describe in detail how product is to be processed and produced. Often the Six Sigma project team will discover better ways of doing things. If manufacturing plans are not changed, the new and improved approach is likely to be lost due to personnel turnovers, etc. In organizations that have no manufacturing plans, the Six Sigma project team should develop them, at least for products and processes developed as part of the project. Note: this should not be considered scope creep or scope drift because it is directly related to the team's goals. However, it will be better still if the team can obtain a permanent policy change to make manufacturing planning a matter of policy (see above).

- *Revise accounting systems.* Six Sigma projects take a value-stream perspective of business systems, i.e., a global approach. However, many cost accounting systems (such as activity-based costing) look at local activities in isolation. If kept in place, these accounting systems produce perverse incentives that will eventually undo all of the good the team has done by breaking the integrated value-delivery process into a series of competing fiefdoms. Throughput accounting is recommended (Goldratt, 1990).

- *Revise budgets.* Improvements mean that more can be done with less. Budgets should be adjusted accordingly. However, the general rule of free markets should also be kept in mind: capital flows to the most efficient. I.e., don't cut the budgets of those who succeed.

- *Revise manpower forecasts.* Toyota's Taiichi Ohno, the creator of Lean Production, says that he isn't interested in labor savings, only in workforce savings. In other words, if as a result of a Six Sigma project the same number of units can be produced with fewer people, this should be reflected in staffing requirements. I hasten to point out, however, that research shows that Six Sigma and Total Quality firms increase employment at roughly triple the rate of non-Six Sigma firms. Greater efficiency, higher quality, and faster cycle times allow firms to create more value for customers. Investors, employees, and other stakeholders benefit. Still, resources should be directed to activities that need them.

- *Change information systems* (e.g., MRP, inventory requirements, etc.). Much of what occurs in the organization is not touched by humans. For example:

  - A purchase order might be issued automatically when inventories for a part reach a certain level. However, a Six Sigma project may have eliminated the need for safety stock.

  - An MRP system may generate a schedule based on cycle times rendered obsolete by Six Sigma improvements.

When Six Sigma projects change the underlying relationships on which the automated information systems are based, programs should be modified to reflect this.

The team members should brainstorm to expand this list with ideas from their own organization. The ideas obtained should be used to develop a process control plan that will ensure that the organization continues to enjoy the benefits of the Six Sigma project. A detailed business process change control plan should be prepared and placed within the *Planner* in the Appendix (p. 214).

Worksheet 69. Additional Business Process Change Control Mechanisms

Change Control Mechanism	Changes	Business Process Control Plan Reference
Policy Changes		
New Standards		
Procedure Changes		
Modified Quality Appraisal and Audit Criteria		
Pricing and Bid Model Changes		
Engineering Drawing Changes		
Work Planning Changes		

Change Control Mechanism	Changes	Business Process Control Plan Reference
Budget Revisions		
Accounting Systems Changes		
Workforce Changes		
Information Systems Changes		

Figure 27. Control Gate Criteria

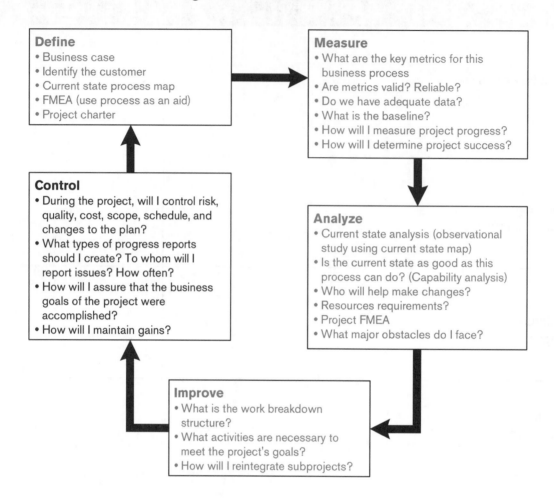

Define
- Business case
- Identify the customer
- Current state process map
- FMEA (use process as an aid)
- Project charter

Measure
- What are the key metrics for this business process
- Are metrics valid? Reliable?
- Do we have adequate data?
- What is the baseline?
- How will I measure project progress?
- How will I determine project success?

Control
- During the project, will I control risk, quality, cost, scope, schedule, and changes to the plan?
- What types of progress reports should I create? To whom will I report issues? How often?
- How will I assure that the business goals of the project were accomplished?
- How will I maintain gains?

Analyze
- Current state analysis (observational study using current state map)
- Is the current state as good as this process can do? (Capability analysis)
- Who will help make changes?
- Resources requirements?
- Project FMEA
- What major obstacles do I face?

Improve
- What is the work breakdown structure?
- What activities are necessary to meet the project's goals?
- How will I reintegrate subprojects?

Chapter 7
A Tutorial on Project Selection and Management

The best Six Sigma projects begin not inside the business but outside it, focused on answering the question: How can we make the customer more competitive? What is critical to the customer's success? Learning the answer to that question and learning how to provide the solution is the only focus we need.

—Jack Welch, CEO, General Electric

I made a number of assumptions in writing *The Six Sigma Project Planner*. One assumption was that the user of the *Planner* was a Black Belt or Green Belt who had received training in the tools and techniques of Six Sigma, including project management training. Another assumption was that the reader was provided with a candidate project by the organization's leadership. The *Planner* is designed to help such users determine if the project is feasible and, if so, to execute the project's charter.

My experience in coaching many people on projects is that the level of understanding individuals bring to the project is highly variable, even if they have received adequate training. Given this state of affairs, it seems reasonable to provide background materials as part of the *Planner,* to help those who need a refresher on the fundamentals of project selection and tracking results. This is not intended to be a substitute for in-depth study of the subject, but it should prove useful to many users. I restrict my discussion to subjects directly related to project selection and management. For a complete discussion of Six Sigma topics, I refer you to my text, *The Six Sigma Handbook*.

Projects are the core activity driving change in the Six Sigma organization. Although change also takes place due to other efforts, such as *Kaizen*, project-based change is the force that drives breakthrough and cultural transformation. In a typical Six Sigma organization, about 1% of the employees are engaged full time in change activities and each of these change agents will complete between three and seven projects in a year. In addition there are another 5% or so part-time change agents, each of whom will complete about two smaller projects per year. In an organization with 1,000 employees, the mathematics translate to about 50 major projects and 100 smaller projects in any given year. Clearly, learning how to effectively deal with projects is critical to Six Sigma success.

Choosing the Right Projects

Projects must be focused on the *right* goals. This is the responsibility of the senior leadership, e.g., the project sponsor, Six Sigma Executive Council, or equivalent group. Senior leadership is the only group with the authority and perspective to designate cross-functional responsibilities and allow access to interdepartmental resources. Six Sigma projects will impact one of the major stakeholder groups: customers, shareholders, or employees. Although it is possible to calculate the impact of any given project on all three groups, I recommend that projects be evaluated separately for each group. This keeps the analysis relatively simple and ensures that a good stakeholder mix is represented in the project portfolio.

Customer Value Projects

Many, if not most Six Sigma projects are selected because they have a positive impact on customers. To evaluate such projects, one must be able to determine the linkage between business processes and customer-perceived value. Customer-driven organizations, especially process enterprises, focus on customer value as a matter of routine. This focus will generate many Six Sigma customer value projects in the course of strategy deployment. However, in addition to the strategy-based linkage of Six Sigma projects, there is also a need to use customer demands *directly* to generate focused Six Sigma projects. Both approaches are described below.

Learning what customers value is primarily determined by first-hand contact with customers through customer focus groups, interviews, surveys, etc. The connection between customer-perceived value and business processes, or *customer value streams*, is established through business process mapping and quality function deployment (QFD). The Executive Six Sigma Council and project sponsors should carefully review the results of these efforts to locate the "lever points" where Six Sigma projects will have the greatest impact on customer value.

Using QFD to Link Six Sigma Projects to Strategies

A common problem with Six Sigma is that there is a cognitive disconnect between the Six Sigma projects and top leadership's strategic goals. *Strategy deployment plans* are simple maps showing the linkage between stakeholder satisfaction, strategies, and metrics. However, these maps are inadequate guides to operational personnel trying to relate their activities—including Six Sigma projects—to the vision of their leadership. Unfortunately, more complexity is required to communicate the strategic message throughout the organization all the way to specific Six Sigma projects. We will use QFD for this purpose. An example, based on the strategy deployment plan shown in Figure 28, will be used to illustrate the process.

Figure 28. Strategy Deployment Plan

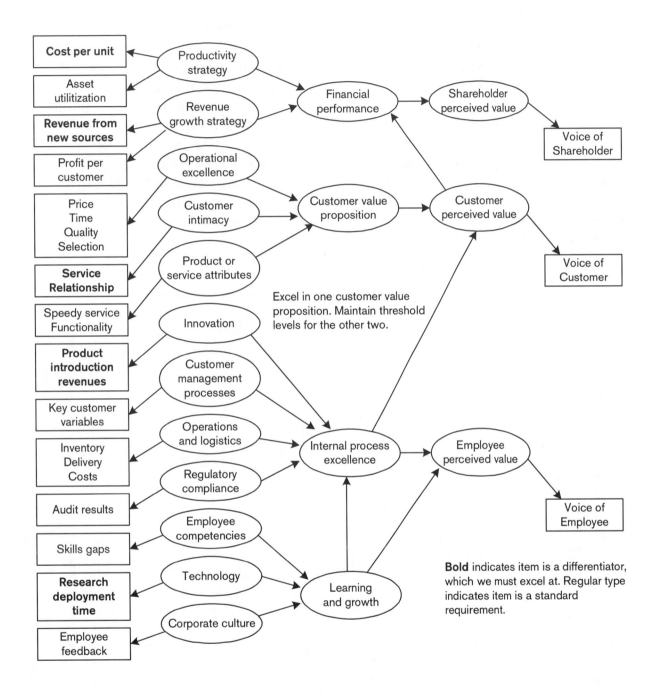

Excel in one customer value proposition. Maintain threshold levels for the other two.

Bold indicates item is a differentiator, which we must excel at. Regular type indicates item is a standard requirement.

The Strategy Deployment Matrix

The first QFD matrix will be based directly on the strategy deployment plan. If you take a closer look at the strategy deployment plan, you'll notice that it fails to show all relationships. For example, the strategy for operational excellence is related to operations and logistics, but the strategy deployment plan doesn't show this (except indirectly through the link between internal process excellence and customer perceived value). Since the purpose of the strategy deployment plan is to present a clear, simple picture of the linkage among leadership's vision, strategy, and metrics, this simplification is acceptable. However, we must go beyond the strategy deployment plan if we are to properly evaluate Six Sigma project candidates. For example, a Six Sigma project addressing inventory levels would have an impact on both strategies, but it wouldn't be possible to measure the impact from the strategy deployment plan alone. QFD will help us make this evaluation explicit. A completed Phase I *strategy deployment matrix* is shown in Figure 29.

Figure 29. Strategy Deployment Matrix

Chart produced using QFD Designer software. Qualsoft, LLC, www.qualisoft.com.

Sorted Strategy Matrix			New product introductions	Revenue from new sources	Customer relationship	R&D deployment time	Inventory turns	Fast service	New product revenues	Fast delivery	Product functionality	Skills audit gaps	CTQs	Asset Utilization	Profit per customer	Price	Cost per unit	Compliance audit score	Employee feedback	Product quality	Shipping & handling costs	Product selection	Area Score (row sum)	Relative Area Performance
Strategy	Financial Performance	Productivity					V						G	V	G		V						29	
		Revenue growth	V	V	G	W			V						V								40	
	Customer Value	Operational excellence					V			V		G	W	W	G	V	G			V	G	V	55	
		Customer intimacy		G	V			G				G	W										15	
		Product attributes	V					V			V					W	W						33	
	Internal Process Excellence	Innovation	V	V		V			V		G												37	
		Customer management processes			V				W				W	V	G								25	
		Operations and logistics					V	V		V			W	G	G						V		41	
		Regulatory compliance																V					9	
	Learning and Growth	Employee competencies		W		W			G	G		V							W	G			21	
		Technology	V	V		V			G		V				G	G							39	
		Corporate culture		W	V							W							W	V			27	
Criteria Performance Target			+50%	20% of total revenues	VOC average > 6.5	-30%	+20%	Top 25%	25% of total	Above industry	All-weather capability	3.5 sigma	4.5 sigma	15% RONA	10% increase	No price increase	-6%	4 sigma	Avg > 6.2	Top 20%	-10%	5% improvement		
Criteria Score			36	34	28	24	27	22	20	19	19	17	16	15	14	14	13	12	12	10	10	9		
Strategic Importance Score			E	E	E	E	L	L	L	L	L	L	L	L	L	L	L	L	L	L	L	L		
Relative Metric Weight																								

168

The process for developing the strategy deployment matrix is as follows:

1. Create a matrix of the strategies and metrics.

2. Determine the strength of the relationship between each strategy and each metric.

3. Calculate a weight indicating the relative importance of the metric.

To begin, we create a matrix where the rows are the strategies (what we want to accomplish) and the columns are the dashboard metrics (how we will operationalize the strategies and monitor progress). Note that this is the typical what-how QFD matrix layout, just with a different spin. In each cell (intersection of a row and a column), we will place a symbol assigning a weight to the relationship between the row and the column. The weights and symbols used are shown in Figure 30.

Figure 30. QFD Relationship Weights and Symbols

Relationship Description	Weight	Symbol
Strong relationship	9	◉
Moderate relationship	3	○
Some relationship	1	△
Differentiator metric	5	●
Key requirement metric	1	✓

The weights are somewhat arbitrary and you can choose others if you desire. These particular values increase more or less exponentially, which places a high emphasis on strong relationships, the idea being that we are looking for clear priorities. Weights of 1-2-3 would treat the different relationship strengths as increasing linearly. Choose the weighting scheme you feel best fits your needs.

After the relationships have been determined for each cell, we are ready to calculate scores for each row. Remember: the rows represent strategies.

For example, the first row represents our productivity strategy. The strategy deployment plan indicated that the productivity strategy was operationalized by the metrics "cost per unit" and "asset utilization" and a strong relationship (◉) is shown between these metrics and the productivity strategy. However, QFD analysis also shows a strong relationship between this strategy and inventory turns, which affects asset utilization. Critical to quality (CTQ) and profit per customer are somewhat related to this strategy. To get an overall score for the metrics relating to the productivity strategy, sum the weights across the first row; the answer is 29. These row (strategy) weights provide information on the how well the dashboards measure the strategies. A zero would indicate that the strategy isn't measured at all. However, a relatively low score doesn't necessarily indicate a problem. For example, the regulatory compliance strategy has a score of 9, but that comes from a strong relationship between the regulatory compliance audit and the strategy. Since the audit covers all major compliance issues, it's entirely possible that this single metric is sufficient.

The columns represent the metrics on the top-level dashboard, although only the differentiator metrics will be monitored on an ongoing basis. The metric's target is shown at the bottom of each column in the "How" portion of the matrix. QFD provides a reality check on the targets. As you will see, QFD links the targets to specific Six Sigma activities designed to achieve them. In the project phase, it is far easier to estimate the impact the projects will have on the metric. If the sum of the project impacts isn't enough to reach the target, either more effort is needed or the target must be revised. Don't forget: there's more to achieving goals than Six Sigma. Don't hesitate to use QFD to link the organization's other activities to the goals.

The strategy is based on leadership's vision for the company, which in this example is that it be the supplier of choice for customers who want state-of-the-art products customized to their demanding requirements. To achieve this vision, the leadership will focus its strategy on four key differentiators: new product introductions, revenue from new sources, intimate customer relationship, and R&D deployment time.

With our chosen weighting scheme differentiator, columns have a strategic importance score of 5, indicated with a ● in the row labeled "Strategic Importance Score." These are the metrics that leadership will watch carefully throughout the year and the goals for them are set very high. Other metrics must meet less demanding standards and will be brought to the attention of leadership only on an exception basis. The row labeled "Relative Metric Weight" is the product of the "Criteria Score" times the "Strategic Importance Score" as a percentage for each column. The four differentiator metrics have the highest relative scores, while product selection (i.e., having a wide variety of standard products for the customer to choose from) is the lowest.

It is vital when using QFD to focus on only the most important columns!

Columns identified with a ✔ in the row labeled "Strategic Importance Score" are not part of the organization's differentiation strategy. This isn't to say that they are unimportant. What it means is that targets for these metrics will probably be set at or near their historical levels as indicated by process behavior charts. The goals will be to maintain these metrics, rather than to drive them to new heights. An organization has only limited resources to devote to change; these resources must be focused if they are to make a difference that customers and shareholders will notice. This organization's complete dashboard has 20 metrics, which can hardly be considered a "focus." By limiting attention to the four differentiators, the organization can pursue the strategy that its leadership believes will make it stand out in the marketplace for customer and shareholder dollars.[1]

---

[1] The key requirements probably won't require explicit support plans. However, if they do, QFD can be used to evaluate the plans. Key requirements QFD should be handled separately.

Deploying Differentiators to Operations

QFD most often fails because the matrices grow until the analysis becomes burdensome. As the matrix grows like Topsy and becomes unwieldy, the team performing QFD begins to sense the lack of focus being documented by the QFD matrix. Soon, interest begins to wane and eventually the effort grinds to a halt. This too is avoided by eliminating ✔key requirements from the strategy deployment matrix. We will create a second-level matrix linked only to the differentiators. This matrix (shown in Figure 31) relates the differentiator dashboard metrics to departmental support strategies.

Figure 31. Phase II Matrix: Differentiators

Chart produced using QFD Designer software. Qualsoft, LLC, www.qualisoft.com.

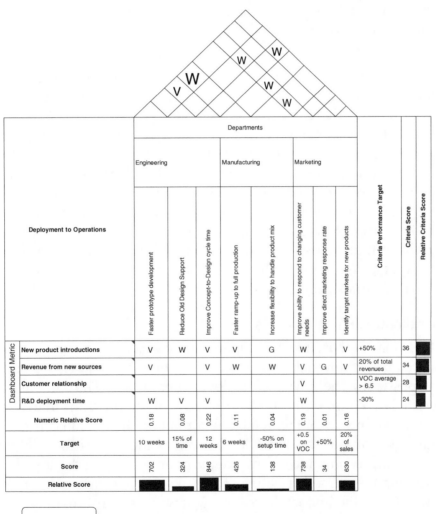

To keep things simple, we show the strategy linkage for only three departments: engineering, manufacturing, and marketing; each department can prepare its own QFD matrix. Notice that the four differentiator metric columns in Figure 29 appear as rows in the matrix in Figure 31. The rows are the QFD "whats." The software automatically brings over the criteria performance target, criteria scores, and relative criteria scores for each row. If you're using another method, you'll need to do this manually. This information is used to evaluate the strategy support plans for the three departments.

The support plans for the three departments are shown as columns, the QFD "hows," or how these three departments plan to implement the strategies. The relationship between the whats and hows is determined as described above for Figure 29. For each column, the value of the each relationship is multiplied by the row Criteria Score and the results of those calculations are summed and shown in the Score row near the bottom of the chart. This information will be used to select and prioritize Six Sigma projects in the next phase of the QFD.

Figure 31 also has a "roof," which shows correlations among the whats. This is useful in identifying related Six Sigma projects, either within the same department or in different departments. For example, there is a strong relationship between the two engineering activities: "faster prototype development" and "improve concept-to-design cycle time." Perhaps faster prototype development should be a subproject under the broader heading of "improve concept-to-design cycle time." This also suggests that a project described as "improve concept-to-design cycle time" may be too large in scope. The marketing strategy of "improve ability to respond to changing customer needs" is correlated with three projects in engineering and manufacturing. When a strategy support plan involves many cross-functional projects, it may indicate the existence of a core process. This suggests a need for high-level sponsorship or the designation of a process owner to coordinate projects.

Deploying Operations Plans to Projects

Figure 32 is a QFD matrix that links the department plans to Six Sigma projects. (In reality this may require additional flow-down steps, but the number of steps should be kept as small as possible.) The rows are the department plans. The software also carried over the numeric relative score from the bottom row of the previous matrix, which is a measure of the relative impact of the department plan on the overall differentiator strategy. The far right column, labeled "Goal Score," is the sum of the relationships for the row. For this example, only the top five department plans are deployed to Six Sigma projects. By summing the numeric relative scores, we can determine that these five plans account for 86% of the impact. In reality, you will also capture only the biggest hitters, although there's nothing magic about the number five.

There are three Black Belts shown and eight projects. Each project is shown as a column in the matrix. The relationship between the project and each departmental plan is shown in the matrix. The bottom row shows the "Project Impact Score," which is the sum of the relationships for the project's column times the row's numeric relative score.

Figure 32. Phase III Matrix: Six Sigma Projects

Chart produced using QFD Designer software. Qualsoft, LLC, www.qualisoft.com.

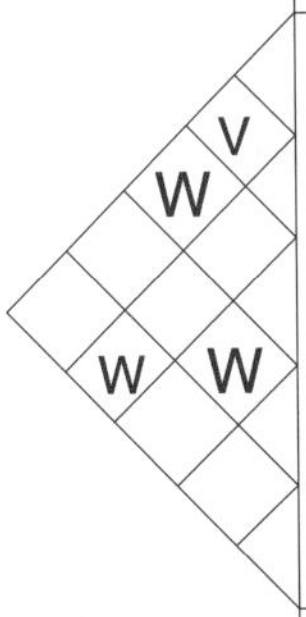

Deployment to Projects			Black Belt: Mike L: Pin manufacturing capability	Black Belt: Mike L: Customer requirements -> Eng requirements	Black Belt: Lori S: Reduced BP errors	Black Belt: Lori S: Reduced prototype -> production model design time	Black Belt: Lori S: Reduce supplier bid cycle time	Black Belt: Nguyet H: Reduce customer bid cycle time	Black Belt: Nguyet H: Reduce customer "non-responsive" complaints	Black Belt: Nguyet H: Reduce part-count in new product	Target	Numeric Relative Score	Goal Score
Departments	Engineering	Faster prototype development		W		V	G			W	10 weeks	0.18	**16**
		Improve Concept-to-Design cycle time		V	W	V				V	12 weeks	0.22	**30**
	Manufacturing	Faster ramp-up to full production		G	W	W	V			V	6 weeks	0.11	**25**
	Marketing	Improve ability to respond to changing customer needs		W			G	V	V		+0.5 on VOC	0.19	**22**
		Identify target markets for new products									20% of sales to new markets	0.16	**0**
Project Impact Score			**0.00**	**3.22**	**0.99**	**3.96**	**1.37**	**1.73**	**1.73**	**3.53**			

Interpretation

Since the numeric relative scores are linked to department plans, which are linked to differentiator metrics, which are linked to strategies, the "Project Impact Score" measures the project's impact on the strategy. Through the strategy deployment plan, we can trace the need for the project all the way back to stakeholders (Figure 33). This logical thread provides those engaged in Six Sigma projects with an anchor to reality and the meaning behind their activities.

The "Goal Score" column can also be used to determine the support Six Sigma provides for each department plan. Note that the marketing plan to "identify target markets for new products" isn't receiving any support at all from Six Sigma projects (assuming, of course, that these eight projects are all of the Six Sigma projects). This may be OK or it may not be. It all depends on how important the plan is to the strategic objectives and what other activities are being pursued to implement the plan. The Executive Six Sigma Council may wish to examine the project QFD matrices to determine if action is necessary to reallocate Six Sigma resources.

Figure 33. Linkage Between Six Sigma Projects and Stakeholders

The "Project Impact Score" row is useful in much the same way. The column scores can be rank-ordered to see which projects have the greatest impact on the strategy. It is also useful in identifying irrelevant projects. The project Mike L is pursuing to improve "pin manufacturing capability" has no impact on any of the departmental plans. Unless this project has an impact on some other strategy support plan that isn't shown in the QFD matrix, it should probably be abandoned as a Six Sigma project. The project may still be something the manufacturing or quality department wants to pursue, perhaps to meet a goal for a key requirement. However, as a general rule, Six Sigma projects requiring a Black Belt should focus on plans that have a direct linkage to differentiator strategies. The role of Black Belts as change agents requires that they limit their scope accordingly.

Using Customer Demands to Design for Six Sigma

Once customers have made their demands known, it is important that these be converted into internal requirements and specifications. The term "translation" is used to describe this process, because the activity literally involves interpreting the words in one language (the customers') into those of another (the employees').

For example, regarding the door of her automobile, the customer might say, "I want the door to close completely when I push it, but I don't want it swinging closed from just the wind." The engineers working with this requirement must convert it into engineering terminology, such as pounds of force required to move the door from an open to a closed position, the angle of the door when it's opened, and so on.

Care must be taken to maintain the customers' intent throughout the development of internal requirements. The same concept applies to service and transactional operations. For example, customers might say, "I want my call answered quickly" or "I want convenient parking." Customer requirements should drive management systems development. The purpose of specifications is to transmit the voice of the customers throughout the organization.

In addition to the issue of maintaining the voice of the customers by tracking their demands as they flow through the system, there is the related issue of the importance assigned to each demand by the customers. Design of products and services always involves tradeoffs: as vehicle weight increases, gasoline economy suffers but safety improves. The importance of each criterion must be determined from the customers' perspective. When different customers assign different levels of importance to the same criteria, design decisions are further complicated. It becomes difficult to choose from competing designs in the face of such ambiguity and customer-to-customer variation. Add to this the differences between internal personnel and objectives—department vs. department, designer vs. designer, cost vs. quality, etc.—and the problem of choosing a design alternative quickly can become unwieldy. In dealing with the complexity, it helps to have a rigorous process for deciding on an alternative.

Structured Decision-Making

The first step is to identify the goal of the design activity. For example, let's say you're the owner of the product development process for a company that sells software to help individuals manage their personal finances. The product, let's call it DollarWise, is dominant in its market and your company is well respected by its customers and by competitors, in large part because of this product's reputation. The business is profitable and the leadership naturally wants to maintain this pleasant set of circumstances and to build on it for the future. The organization has committed itself to a strategy of keeping DollarWise the leader in its market segment so it can capitalize on its reputation by launching additional new products directed toward other financially oriented customer groups, such as small businesses. They have determined that product development is a core process for deploying this strategy.

The process owner or business process executive has control of the budget for product development, including the resources to upgrade the existing product. Although it is still considered the best personal financial software available, DollarWise is getting a little long in the tooth and the competition has steadily closed the technical gap. You believe that a major product upgrade is necessary and want to focus your resources on those things that matter most to customers. Thus, your goal is:

Goal: Determine where to focus product upgrade resources

Through a variety of "listening posts" (e.g., personal contact, focus groups, user laboratories, Internet forums, trade show interviews, conference hospitality suites, surveys, letters, technical support feedback, etc.), you have determined that customers make comments like the following:

- Can I link a DollarWise total to a report in my word processor?

- I have a high-speed connection and I'd like to be able to download big databases of stock information to analyze with DollarWise.

- I like shortcut keys so I don't have to always click around in menus.

- I only have a 56K connection and DollarWise is slow on it.

- I use the Internet to pay bills through my bank. I'd like to do this using DollarWise instead of going to my bank's Web site.

- I want an interactive tutorial to help me get started.

- I want printed documentation.

- I want the installation to be simple.

- I want the user interface to be intuitive.

- I want to be able to download and reconcile my bank statements.

175

- I want to be able to upgrade over the Internet.

- I want to manage my stock portfolio and track my ROI.

- I'd like to have the reports I run every month saved and easy to update.

- It's a pain to set up the different drilldowns every time I want to analyze my spending.

- It's clunky to transfer information between DollarWise and Excel.

- When I have a minor problem, I'd like to have easy-to-use self-help available on the Internet or in the help file.

- When it's a problem I can't solve myself, I want reasonably priced, easy-to-reach technical support.

- You should make patches and bug fixes available free on the Internet.

The first step in using this laundry list of comments is to see if there's an underlying structure embedded in them. If these many comments address only a few issues, it will simplify the problem of understanding what the customer actually wants from the product.

While there are statistical tools to help accomplish this task (e.g., structural equation modeling, principal components analysis, factor analysis), they are quite advanced and require that substantial data be collected using well-designed and thoroughly tested survey instruments. A simple alternative is to create an *affinity diagram*, which is a simple procedure used to identify groupings of similar items. After creating the affinity diagram, the following structure is identified:

1. "Easy to learn."

    1.1. I want the installation to be simple.

    1.2. I want an interactive tutorial to help me get started.

    1.3. I want printed documentation.

    1.4. I want the user interface to be intuitive.

2. "Easy to use quickly after I've learned it well."

    2.1. I like shortcut keys so I don't have to always click around in menus.

    2.2. I'd like to have the reports I run every month saved and easy to update.

    2.3. It's a pain to set up the different drilldowns every time I want to analyze my spending.

3. "Internet connectivity."

    3.1. I use the Internet to pay bills through my bank. I'd like to do this using DollarWise instead of going to my bank's Web site.

    3.2. I only have a 56K connection and DollarWise is slow on it.

3.3. I have a high-speed connection and I'd like to be able to download big databases of stock information to analyze with DollarWise.

3.4. I want to be able to download and reconcile my bank statements.

3.5. I want to manage my stock portfolio and track my ROI.

4. "Works well with other software I own."

4.1. It's clunky to transfer information between DollarWise and Excel.

4.2. Can I link a DollarWise total to a report in my word processor?

5. "Easy to maintain."

5.1. I want to be able to upgrade over the Internet.

5.2. You should make patches and bug fixes available free on the Internet.

5.3. When I have a minor problem, I'd like to have easy-to-use self-help available on the Internet or in the help file.

5.4. When it's a problem I can't solve myself, I want reasonably priced, easy-to-reach technical support.

The reduced customer demand model, which is illustrated graphically in Figure 34 shows that five key factors are operationalized by the many different customer comments.

Figure 34. Customer Demand Model

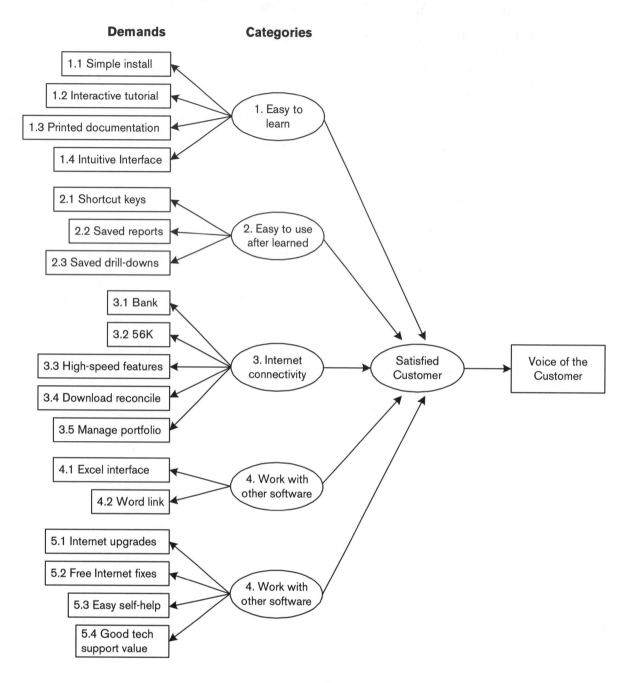

Next, we must determine importance placed on each item by customers. There are a number of ways to do this.

- Have customers assign importance weights using a numerical scale (e.g., "How important is 'Easy self-help' on a scale between 1 and 10?").

- Have customers assign importance using a subjective scale (e.g., unimportant, important, very important, etc.).

- Have customers "spend" $100 by allocating it among the various items. In these cases, it is generally easier for the customer to first allocate the $100 to the major categories, then allocate another $100 to items within each category.

- Have customers evaluate a set of hypothetical product offerings and indicate their preference for each product by ranking the offerings, assigning a 'likely to buy' rating, etc. The product offerings include a mix of items carefully selected from the list of customer demands. The items are selected in such a way that the relative value the customer places on each item in the offering can be determined from the preference ranks. This is known as *conjoint analysis*, an advanced technique that is covered in most texts on marketing statistics.

- Have customers evaluate the items in pairs, assigning a preference rating to one of the items in each pair or deciding that both items in a pair are equally important. This is less tedious if the major categories are evaluated first, then the items within each category. The evaluation can use either numeric values or descriptive labels that are converted to numeric values. The pairwise comparisons can be analyzed to derive item weights using a method known as the analytic hierarchy process (AHP) to determine the relative importance assigned to all of the items.

All of the above methods have their advantages and disadvantages. The simple methods are easy to use but less powerful (i.e., the assigned weights are less likely to reflect actual weights). The more advanced conjoint method requires special skills to analyze and interpret properly. We will illustrate the use of AHP for our hypothetical software product. AHP is a powerful technique that has been proven in a wide variety of applications, yet it can be analyzed with spreadsheet software. In addition to its use in determining customer importance values, it is useful for decision-making in general.

Category Importance Weights

We begin our analysis by making pairwise comparison at the top level. The affinity analysis identified five categories: "easy to learn," "easy to use quickly after I've learned it," "Internet connectivity," "works well with other software I own," and "easy to maintain." Arrange these items in a matrix as shown in Figure 35.

Figure 35. Matrix of Categories for Pairwise Comparisons

Created using Expert Choice 2000 Software, www.expertchoice.com.[2]

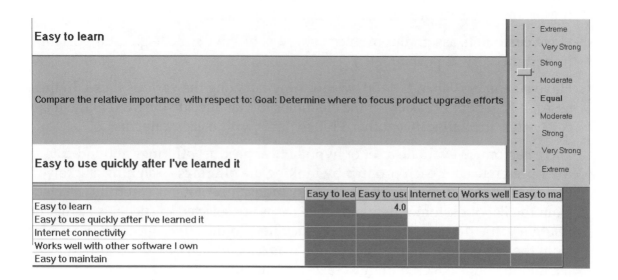

For our analysis, we will assign verbal labels to our pairwise comparisons; the verbal responses will be converted into numerical values for analysis. Customers usually find it easier to assign verbal labels than numeric labels. All comparisons are made relative to the customers' goal of determining which product they will buy, which we assume is synonymous with our goal of determining where to focus product upgrade efforts. The highlighted cell in the matrix compares the 'easy to learn' attribute and the 'easy to use quickly after I've learned it' attribute. The customer must determine which is more important to him or her or if the two attributes are of equal importance. In this example, our customer indicates that 'easy to learn' is moderately to strongly preferred over 'easy to use quickly after I've learned it' and the AHP software has placed a +4 in the cell comparing these two attributes. (The scale goes from –9 to +9, with 'equal' being identified as a 1.) The remaining attributes are compared one by one, resulting in the matrix shown in Figure 36.

---

[2] Although the analysis is easier with special software, you can obtain a good approximation using a spreadsheet. See the Appendix for details.

Figure 36. Completed Top-Level Comparison Matrix

	Easy to learn	Easy to use quickly	Internet connectivity	Works well with other software	Easy to maintain
Easy to learn		4	1	3	1
Easy to use quickly after I've learned it			0.20	0.33	0.25
Internet connectivity				3	3
Works well with other software I own					0.33
Easy to maintain	Incon: 0.05				

Numerically, the importance weights for each attribute are as follow:[3]

- Easy to learn: 0.264 (26.4%)

- Easy to use quickly after I've learned it: 0.054 (5.4%)

- Internet connectivity: 0.358 (35.8%)

- Works well with other software I own: 0.105 (10.5%)

- Easy to maintain: 0.218 (21.8%)

These relative importance weights can be used in QFD as well as in the AHP process that we are illustrating here. In our allocation of effort, we will want to emphasize those attributes with high importance weights over those with lower weights.

Subcategory Importance Weights

The process used for obtaining category importance weights is repeated for the items within each category. E.g., the items 'interactive tutorial,' 'good documentation,' and 'intuitive interface' are compared pairwise within the category 'Easy to Learn.' This provides weights that indicate the importance of each item on the category. For example, within the 'Easy to Learn' category, the customer weights might be:

- Interactive tutorial: 11.7%

- Good documentation: 20.0%

- Intuitive interface: 68.3%

If there were additional levels below these subcategories, the process would be repeated for them. For example, the "intuitive interface" subcategory might be subdivided into "number of menus," "number of submenus," "menu items easily understood," etc. The

---

[3] See the Appendix for an example of how to derive approximate importance weights using Microsoft Excel.

greater the level of detail, the easier the translation of the customer demands into internal specifications. The tradeoff is that the process quickly becomes tedious and may end up asking the customers for input they aren't qualified to provide. Customers are notoriously impatient with providing detailed information about their likes and dislikes! In the case of this example, we'd probably stop at the second level.

Global Importance Weights

The subcategory weights just obtained tell us how much importance the item has with respect to the *category*, not with respect to the ultimate goal. Thus, they are often called *local importance weights*. However, the subcategory weights don't tell us the impact of the item on the overall goal, which is called its *global impact*. Global impact is calculated by multiplying the subcategory item weight by the weight of the category in which the item resides. The global weights for our example are shown in Table 10 in descending order.

Table 10. Local and Global Importance Weights

Category	Subcategory	Local Weight	Global Weight
Easy to learn	Intuitive interface	68.3%	18.0%
Internet connectivity	Online billpay	43.4%	15.5%
Internet connectivity	Download statements	23.9%	8.6%
Internet connectivity	Download investment information	23.9%	8.6%
Works well with other software	Hotlinks to spreadsheet	75.0%	7.9%
Easy to maintain	Free Internet patches	35.7%	7.8%
Easy to maintain	Great, free self-help technical assistance on the Internet	30.8%	6.7%
Easy to learn	Good documentation	20.0%	5.3%
Easy to maintain	Reasonably priced advanced technical support	20.0%	4.4%
Internet connectivity	Works well at 56K	8.9%	3.2%
Easy to learn	Interactive tutorial	11.7%	3.1%
Easy to maintain	Automatic Internet upgrades	13.5%	2.9%
Works well with other software	Edit reports in word processor	25.0%	2.6%
Easy to use quickly after I've learned it	Savable frequently used reports	43.4%	2.3%
Easy to use quickly after I've learned it	Shortcut keys	23.9%	1.3%
Easy to use quickly after I've learned it	Short menus showing only frequently used commands	23.9%	1.3%
Easy to use quickly after I've learned it	Macro capability	8.9%	0.5%

The global importance weights are most useful for the purpose of allocating resources to the overall goal which, you may recall, is *Determine where to focus product upgrade efforts*. For our example, Internet connectivity obviously has a huge customer impact. 'Easy to use quickly after I've learned it' has relatively low impact. 'Easy to learn' is dominated by one item: the user interface. These weights will be used to assess different proposed upgrade designs and plans.

Each plan will be evaluated on each subcategory item and assigned a value depending on how well it addresses the item. The values will be multiplied by the global weights to arrive at an overall score for the plan. The scores can be rank-ordered to provide a list that the process owner can use when making resource allocation decisions. Or, more proactively, the information can be used to develop a plan that emphasizes the most important customer demands.

Table 11 shows part of a table that assesses project plans using the global weights. The numerical rating used in the table is 0 = No Impact, 1 = Some Impact, 3 = Moderate Impact, 5 = High Impact. Since the global weights sum to 1 (100%), the highest possible score is 5. Of the five plans evaluated, Plan C has the highest score. It can be seen that Plan C has a high impact on the six most important customer demands. It has at least a moderate impact on 10 of the top 11 items, with the exception of 'Reasonably priced advanced technical support.' These items account for almost 90% of the customer demands.

Table 11. Example of Using Global Weights in Assessing Alternatives

ITEM	Plan Customer Impact Score	Intuitive interface	Online billpay	Download statements	Download investment information	Hotlinks to spreadsheet	Free Internet patches	Great, free self-help technical assistance on the Internet	Good documentation	Reasonably priced advanced technical support	Works well at 56K	Interactive tutorial
GLOBAL WEIGHT		18.0%	15.5%	8.6%	8.6%	7.9%	7.8%	6.7%	5.3%	4.4%	3.2%	3.1%
Plan A	3.57	3	5	1	1	3	3	4	5	5	5	5
Plan B	2.99	1	1	1	3	3	5	5	5	5	5	5
Plan C	4.15	5	5	5	5	5	5	3	3	1	3	3
Plan D	3.36	3	3	3	3	3	3	3	5	5	5	5
Plan E	2.30	5	0	0	0	5	5	1	1	0	1	1

The plan's customer impact score is, of course, only one input into the decision-making process. The rigor involved usually makes the score a very valuable piece of information. It is also possible to use the same approach to incorporate other information, such as cost, timetable, feasibility, etc. into the final decision. The process owner would make pairwise comparisons of the different inputs (customer impact score, cost, feasibility, etc.) to assign weights to them and then use the weights to determine an overall plan score. Note that this process is a mixture of AHP and QFD.

Shareholder Value Projects

Six Sigma provides a "double whammy" by addressing both efficiency and revenues. Revenue is impacted by improving the customer value proposition, which allows organizations to charge premium prices for superior quality or to keep prices competitive and increase sales volume and market share. Improved efficiency is achieved by reducing the cost of poor quality, reducing cycle time, or eliminating waste in business processes. To determine which Six Sigma projects address the issue of business process efficiency evaluate the high-level business process maps (including SIPOCs) and flowcharts.

Other Six Sigma Projects

Some Six Sigma projects address intangibles, such as employee morale, regulatory concerns, or environmental issues. These projects can be just as important as those that address customer or shareholder value.

Analyzing Project Candidates

You now have a list of candidate Six Sigma projects. The next task is to select a subset of these projects to fund and staff. Projects cost money, take time, and disrupt normal operations and standard routines. For these reasons, projects designed to improve processes should be limited to processes that are important to the enterprise. Furthermore, projects should be undertaken only when success is highly likely.

Feasibility is determined by considering the scope and cost of a project and the support it receives from the process owner. In this section, a number of techniques and approaches are presented to help identify those projects that will be chosen for Six Sigma.

Other Methods of Identifying Promising Projects

Projects should be selected to support the organization's overall strategy and mission. Because of this global perspective, most projects involve the efforts of several different functional areas. Not only do individual quality projects tend to cut across organizational boundaries, different projects are often related to one another. To effectively manage this complexity, it is necessary to integrate the planning and execution of projects across the entire enterprise. One way to accomplish this is QFD, which is discussed in detail above. In addition to QFD and the scoring method included in the *Planner* (see Worksheet 3, Six Sigma Project Evaluation, p. 9) a number of other procedures are presented here to help identify a project's potential worth.

Using Pareto Analysis to Identify Six Sigma Project Candidates

The *Pareto principle* refers to the fact that a small percentage of processes cause a large percentage of the problems. The Pareto principle is useful in narrowing a list of choices to those few projects that offer the greatest potential. When using Pareto analysis, keep in mind that there may be hidden "pain signals." Initially, problems create pain signals such as schedule disruptions and customer complaints. Often these *symptoms* are treated rather than their underlying "diseases." For example, if quality problems cause schedule slippages that lead to customer complaints, the "solution" might be to keep a large inventory and sort the good from the bad. The result is that the schedule is met and customers stop complaining, but at huge cost. These opportunities are often greater than those currently causing "pain," but they are now built into business systems and therefore very difficult to see. One solution to the hidden problem phenomenon is to focus on processes rather than symptoms. Some guidelines for identifying dysfunctional processes for potential improvement are shown in Table 12.

Table 12. Dysfunctional Process Symptoms and Underlying Diseases

Symptom	Disease	Cure
Extensive information exchange, data redundancy, rekeying	Arbitrary fragmentation of a natural process	Discover why people need to communicate with each other so often; integrate the process
Inventory, buffers, and other assets stockpiled	System slack to cope with uncertainty	Remove the uncertainty
High ratio of checking and control to value-added work (excessive test and inspection, internal controls, audits, etc.)	Fragmentation	Eliminate the fragmentation, integrate processes
Rework and iteration	Inadequate feedback in a long work process	Process control
Complexity, exceptions, and special causes	Accretion onto a simple base	Uncover original "clean" process and create new process(es) for special situations; eliminate excessive standardization of processes

The "symptom" column is useful in identifying problems and setting priorities. The "disease" column focuses attention on the underlying causes of the problem, and the "cure" column is helpful in chartering quality improvement project teams and preparing mission statements.

Prioritizing Projects with the Pareto Priority Index

After a serious search for improvement opportunities, the organization's leaders will probably find that there are more projects to pursue than resources. The Pareto Priority Index (PPI) is a simple way of prioritizing these opportunities. The PPI is calculated as follows (*Six Sigma Handbook*, p. 229):

$$PPI = \frac{\text{Savings} \times \text{probability of success}}{\text{Cost} \times \text{time to completion (years)}} \qquad \text{(Equation 1)}$$

A close examination of the PPI equation shows that it is related to return on investment adjusted for probability of success. The inputs are, of course, estimates and the result is totally dependent on the accuracy of the inputs. The resulting number is an index value for a given project. The PPI values allow comparison of various projects. If there are clear standouts, the PPI can make it easier to select a project. Table 13 shows the PPIs for several hypothetical projects.

Table 13. Illustration of the Pareto Priority Index (PPI)

Project	Savings, $ Thousands	Probability	Cost, $ Thousands	Time, Years	PPI
Reduce wave solder defects 50%	$70	0.7	$25	0.75	2.61
NC machine capability improvement	$50	0.9	$20	1.00	2.25
ISO 9001 certification	$150	0.9	$75	2.00	0.90
Eliminate customer delivery complaints	$250	0.5	$75	1.50	1.11
Reduce assembly defects 50%	$90	0.7	$30	1.50	1.40

The PPI indicates that resources be allocated first to reducing wave solder defects, then to improving NC machine capability, and so on. The PPI may not always give such a clear ordering of priorities. When two or more projects have similar PPIs, a judgment must be made on other criteria.

Throughput-Based Project Selection

While careful planning and management of projects is undeniably important, it matters little if the projects being pursued have no impact on the bottom line (throughput). As you will see below, if you choose the wrong projects, it is possible to make apparently big "improvements" in quality and productivity that have no impact whatever on the organization's net profit. Selecting projects to pursue is of critical importance. In this section, we will use the theory of constraints (TOC) to determine which project(s) to pursue.

Theory of Constraints

Every organization has constraints. Constraints come in many forms. When a production or service process has a resource constraint (i.e., it lacks a sufficient quantity of some resource to meet the market demand), then the sequence of improvement projects should be identified using very specific rules. According to Eliyahu M. Goldratt, the rules are:[4]

1. *Identify the system's constraint(s).* Consider a fictitious company that produces only two products, P and Q. The market demand for P is 100 units per week and P sells for $90 per unit. The market demand for Q is 50 units per week and Q sells for $100 per unit. Assume that A, B, C, and D are workers who have different, noninterchangeable skills and that each worker is available for only 2,400 minutes per week (eight hours per day, five days per week). For simplicity, assume that there is no variation, waste, etc. in the process. This process has a constraint, worker B. This fact has profound implications for selecting Six Sigma projects.

Figure 37. A Simple Process with a Constraint

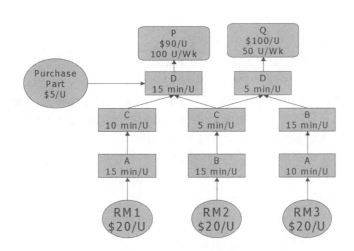

2. *Decide how to exploit the system's constraint(s).* Look for Six Sigma projects that minimize waste of the constraint. For example, if the constraint is the market demand, then we look for Six Sigma projects that provide 100% on-time delivery. Let's not waste anything! If the constraint is a machine, focus on reducing setup time, eliminating scrap, and keeping the machine running as much as possible.

3. *Subordinate everything else to the above decision.* Choose Six Sigma projects to maximize throughput of the constraint. After completing step 2, choose projects to eliminate waste from downstream processes; once the constraint has been utilized to create something, we don't want to lose it due to some downstream blunder. Then choose projects to ensure that the constraint is always supplied with adequate nondefective resources from upstream processes. We pursue upstream processes last because by definition they have slack resources, so

[4]Eliyahu M. Goldratt, *The Haystack Syndrome: Sifting Information Out of the Data Ocean*, North River Press, Great Barrington, MA, 1990, pp. 59-63.

small amounts of waste upstream that are detected before reaching the constraint are less damaging to throughput.

4. *Elevate the system's constraint(s).* Elevate means "lift the restriction." This is step 4, not step 2! Often the projects pursued in steps 2 and 3 will eliminate the constraint. If the constraint continues to exist after performing steps 2 and 3, look for Six Sigma projects that provide additional resources to the constraint. These might involve, for example, purchasing additional equipment or hiring additional workers with a particular skill.

5. *If, in the previous steps, a constraint has been broken, go back to step 1.* There is a tendency for thinking to become conditioned to the existence of the constraint. A kind of mental inertia sets in. If the constraint has been lifted, then you must rethink the entire process from scratch. Returning to step 1 takes you back to the beginning of the cycle.

Comparison of TOC and Traditional Approaches

It can be shown that the TOC approach is superior to the traditional TQM approaches to project selection. For example, consider the data in the table below. If you were to apply Pareto analysis to scrap rates, you would begin with Six Sigma projects that reduced the scrap produced by Worker A. In fact, assuming the optimum product mix, Worker A has about 25% slack time, so the scrap loss can be made up without shutting down Worker B, who is the constraint. The TOC would suggest first addressing the scrap loss of Worker B and the downstream processes C and D—the precise opposite of what Pareto analysis recommends.

Process Scrap Rates

Process	Scrap Rate
A	8%
B	3%
C	5%
D	7%

Of course, before making a decision as to which projects to finance, cost/benefit analyses are still necessary, and the probability of the project succeeding must be estimated. But by using the TOC, you will at least know where to look first for opportunities.

Using Constraint Information to Focus Six Sigma Projects

Applying the TOC strategy described above tells us *where* in the process to focus. Adding CTx information (see Table 14) can help tell us which type of project to focus on, i.e., should we focus on quality, cost or schedule projects? Assume that you have three Six Sigma candidate projects, all focusing on process step B, the constraint. The area addressed is correct, but which project should you pursue first? Let's assume that we learn that one project will primarily improve quality, another cost, and another schedule.

Table 14. Throughput Priority of CTx Projects That Affect the Constraint

Project Type	Discussion
CTQ	Any unit produced by the constraint is especially valuable because, if it is lost as scrap, additional constraint time must be used to replace it or rework it. Since constraint time determines throughput (net profit of the entire system), the loss far exceeds what appears on scrap and rework reports. CTQ projects at the constraint are the highest priority.
CTS	CTS projects can reduce the time it takes the constraint to produce a unit, which means that the constraint can produce more units. This directly impacts throughput. CTS projects at the constraint are the highest priority.
CTC	Since the constraint determines throughput, the cost of the constraint going down is the lost throughput of the *entire system*. This makes the cost of constraint downtime extremely high. The cost of *operating* the constraint is usually miniscule by comparison. Also, CTC projects often have an adverse impact on quality or schedule. Thus, CTC projects at the constraint are low priority.

Does this new information help? Definitely! Take a look at Table 14 to see how this information can be used. Projects in the same priority group are ranked according to their impact on throughput.

The same thought process can be applied to process steps before and after the constraint. The results are shown in Table 15.

Table 15. Project Throughput Priority vs. Project Focus

Focus of Six Sigma Project				
CTx: Characteristic addressed is critical to…		Before the Constraint	At the Constraint	After the Constraint
	Quality (CTQ)	△	◉	◉
	Cost (CTC)	○	△	○
	Schedule (CTS)	△	◉	○

△   Low throughput priority.

○   Moderate throughput priority.

◉   High throughput priority.

Note that Table 15 assumes that projects *before* the constraint do not result in problems *at* the constraint. Remember: impact should always be measured in terms of throughput. If a process upstream from the constraint has an adverse impact on

189

throughput, then it can be considered to be a constraint. For example, if an upstream process *average* yield is enough to feed the constraint on the average, it may still present a problem. An upstream process producing 20 units per day with an average yield of 90% will produce, on average, 18 good units. If the constraint requires 18 units, things will be OK about 50% of the time, but the other 50% of the time things won't be OK. One solution to this problem is to place a work-in-process inventory between the process and the constraint as a safety buffer. Then on those days when the process yield is below 18 units, the inventory can be used to keep the constraint running. However, there is a cost associated with carrying WIP inventory. A Six Sigma project that can improve the yield will reduce or eliminate the need for the inventory and should be considered even if it doesn't impact the constraint directly, assuming the benefit-cost analysis justifies the project. On the other hand, if an upstream process can easily make up any deficit before the constraint needs it, then a project for the process will have a low priority.

Knowing the project's throughput priority will help you make better project selection decisions by helping you select from among project candidates. Of course, the throughput priority is just one input into the project selection process; other factors may lead to a different decision. For example, impact on other projects, a regulatory requirement, a better payoff in the long term, etc.

Multitasking and Project Scheduling

A Six Sigma enterprise will always have more projects to pursue than resources to do them. The fact that resources (usually Black Belts or Green Belts) are scarce means that projects must be scheduled, i.e., some projects must be undertaken earlier than others. In such situations, it is tempting to use *multitasking* of the scarce resource. Multitasking is defined as the assignment of a resource to several priorities during the same period of time. The logic is that by working on several projects or assignments simultaneously, the entire portfolio of work will be done more quickly. However, while this is true for independent resources working independent projects or subprojects in parallel, it is *not* true for a single resource assigned to multiple projects or interdependent tasks within a project.

Consider the following situation. You have three Six Sigma projects: A, B, and C. A single-tasking solution is to first do A, then B, and then C. Here's the single-activity project schedule.

A	B	C
Complete in Week 10	Complete in Week 20	Cmplete in Week 30

If each project takes 10 weeks to complete, then A will be completed in 10 weeks, B in 20 weeks, and C in 30 weeks. The average time to complete the three projects is calculated as follows:

$$\frac{10+20+30}{3} = \frac{60}{3} = 20 \text{ weeks}$$

The average doesn't tell the whole story, either. The benefits will begin as soon as a project is completed; by the end of the 30-week period, project A will have been completed for 20 weeks and project B for 10 weeks.

Now let's consider a multitasking strategy. Here we split our time equally among the three projects in a given 10-week period. That way the sponsor of projects B and C will see activity on their projects much sooner than if we used a single-task approach to scheduling. The new schedule looks like this:

A	B	C	A	B	C	A	B	C

With this multitasking schedule, project A will be completed in 23.3 weeks, project B in 26.7 weeks, and project C will still take 30 weeks. The completion time for project A went from 10 weeks to 23.3 weeks, for project B it went from 20 weeks to 26.7 weeks, and for project C it remained the same, 30 weeks. The overall average completion time went from 20 weeks to 26.67 weeks, a 33% deterioration in average time to complete. And this is a best-case scenario. In real life, there is always some lost time when making the transition from one project to another. The Black Belt has to switch gears, review the next project, get the proper files ready, reawaken sponsors and team members, and so on. This can often take considerable time, which is added to the time needed to complete the projects.

Critical Chain Project Portfolio Management

Critical chain project management avoids the multitasking problem by changing the way the organization manages groups of projects and the way the individual projects are managed.

Managing the Organization's Projects

First, at the organizational level, multitasking of key resources is stopped. People and other resources are allowed to focus on projects one at a time. This means that management must accept responsibility for prioritizing projects and policies must be developed that mandate single-project focus and discourage multitasking. To be successful, the organization must determine its capacity to complete projects. Every organization has more opportunities than it can successfully pursue with finite resources. This means that only a select portfolio of projects should be undertaken in any time interval. The constraining resource is usually a key position in the organization, such as the time available by project sponsors, engineers, programmers, etc. This information can be used to determine organizational capacity and to schedule project start dates according to the availability of the key resource. This is called *project launch synchronization* and the scarce resource that paces the project system is called a *synchronizer resource*.

191

Synchronizer Resource Usage

Critical chain project management does not permit multitasking of scarce resources. Instead, people and equipment that are fully utilized on projects, *synchronizer resources*, are assigned to a sequence of single projects. The sequence of projects is based on enterprise priorities. If a project requires one or more synchronizer resources, it is vital that your project start dates integrate the schedules of these resources. In particular, this will require that those activities that require time from a synchronizer resource (and the project as a whole) stipulate, "Start no earlier than" dates. Although synchronizer resources are protected by capacity buffers and might hypothetically start earlier than specified, the usual practice is to utilize any unplanned excess capacity to allow the organization to pursue additional opportunities, thereby increasing the organization's capacity to complete projects. Note that human resources are defined in terms of the skills required for the activity, not in terms of individual people. In fact, the resource manager should refrain from assigning an activity to an individual until all predecessors have been completed and the activity is ready to begin. This precludes the temptation to multitask as the individual looks ahead and sees the activity start date drawing near.

Project start dates are determined by beginning with the highest-priority project and calculating the end date for the synchronizing resource based on the estimated duration of all activities that require the synchronizing resource. The second-highest-priority project's start date is calculated by adding a capacity buffer to the expected end date of the first project. The third-highest-priority project's start date is based on the completion date of the second, and so on. If, by chance, the synchronizing resource is available before the scheduled start date, the time can be used to increase the organization's capacity to complete more projects. Figure 38 illustrates this strategy.

Summary and Preliminary Project Selection

At this point you have evaluated project candidates using a number of different criteria. You must now rank the projects, and make your preliminary selections. You may use Worksheet 70 to assist you with this. The reason your selections are preliminary is that you lack complete data. As they work the project, Six Sigma project teams will continuously reevaluate it and they may uncover data that will lower or raise the project's priority. The project sponsor is responsible for coordinating changes in priority with the process owners.

Figure 38. Critical Chain Scheduling Illustration

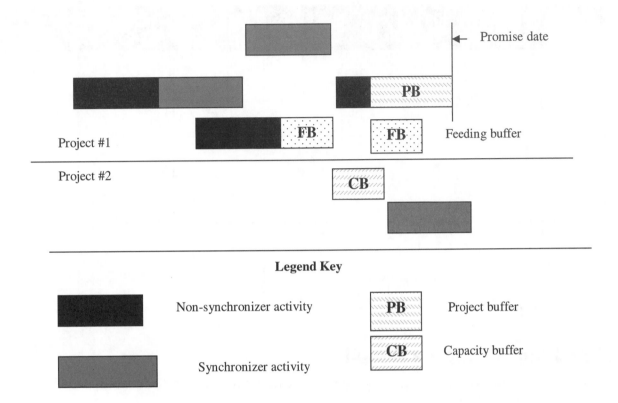

Promise date

Project #1

Project #2

PB

FB   FB   Feeding buffer

CB

Legend Key

Non-synchronizer activity   PB   Project buffer

Synchronizer activity   CB   Capacity buffer

Worksheet 70. Project Assessment Summary

Project Description or ID Number	Project Score	PPI Priority	ROI Priority	Throughput Priority	Comments

Tracking Six Sigma Results

It is vital that information regarding results be accumulated and reported. This is useful for various purposes:

- Evaluating the effectiveness of the Six Sigma project selection system
- Determining the overall return on investment
- Setting budgets
- Appraising individual and group performance
- Setting goals and targets
- Identifying areas where more (or less) emphasis on Six Sigma is indicated
- Helping educate newcomers on the value of Six Sigma
- Answering skeptics
- Quieting cynics

A major difference between Six Sigma and failed programs of the past is the emphasis on tangible, measurable results. Six Sigma advocates make a strong point of the fact that projects are selected to provide a mixture of short- and long-term paybacks that justify the investment and the effort. Unless proof is provided, any statements regarding paybacks are nothing more than empty assertions.

Data storage is becoming so inexpensive that the typical organization can afford to keep fairly massive amounts of data in databases. The limiting factor is the effort needed to enter the data into the system. This is especially important if highly trained change agents such as Master Black Belts, Black Belts, or Green Belts are needed to perform the data entry.

Table 16. Possible Information to Be Captured

- Charter information (title, sponsor, membership, deadline, etc.)
- Description of project in ordinary language
- Project status
- Savings type (hard, soft, cost avoidance, CTQ, etc.)
- Process or unit owner
- Key accounting information (charge numbers, etc.)
- Project originator
- Top-level strategy addressed by project
- Comments, issues
- Lessons learned
- Keywords (for future searches)
- Related documents and links
- Audit trail of changes
- Project task and schedule information

Usually viewing access is restricted to the project data according to role played in the project, position in the organization, etc. Change access is usually restricted to the project sponsor, leader, or Black Belt. However, to the extent possible, it should be easy to "slice-and-dice" this information in various ways. Periodic reports might be created to summarize results according to department, sponsor, Black Belt, etc. The system should also allow ad-hoc views to be easily created, such as the simple list shown in Table 17.

Table 17. A Typical View of Six Sigma Projects

Project ID	Project Title	Status	Black Belt	Sponsor	Due	Savings Type	Total Savings	Costs
76	Cup dipole antenna	Pending approval	J Chambers	Jane Witthers	3/1/04	Hard	$508,000	$5,900
33	Tower assembly	Define	B Dolson	Sal Jones	9/30/03	Hard	$250,000	$25,000
35	SSPA	Completed	N Hepler	Mike Davis	10/31/03	Cost avoidance	$1.3 million	$13,000
37	FCC RFI compliance	Control	M Little	A Langer	9/30/03	Other	NA	$1,500

Financial Results Validation

Claimed Six Sigma financial benefits for every project must be confirmed by experts in accounting or finance. Initial savings estimates may be calculated by Black Belts or sponsors, but final results require at least the concurrence of the finance department. This should be built in from the start. The finance person assigned to work with the team should be listed in the project charter. Without this involvement, the claimed savings are simply not credible. Aside from the built-in bias involved in calculating the benefit created from one's own project, there is the issue of qualifications. The people best qualified to calculate financial benefits are generally those who do such calculations for a living.

This is not to imply that the finance expert's numbers should go unchallenged. If the results appear to be unreasonable, either high or low, then they should be clearly explained in terms the sponsor understands. The Six Sigma leader also has an interest in ensuring that the numbers are valid. Invalid results pose a threat to the viability of the Six Sigma effort itself.

For example, on one project the Black Belt claimed savings of several hundred thousand dollars for "unpaid overtime." A finance person concurred. However, the Six Sigma leader would not accept the savings, arguing quite reasonably that the company hadn't saved anything if it had never paid the overtime. This isn't to say that the project didn't have a benefit, e.g., perhaps morale improved or turnover declined due to the shorter working hours. However, if these are the benefits claimed, then they need to be documented directly, not converted into a dubious dollar savings. Care must be taken to show the benefits properly.

Types of Savings

The accounting or finance department should formally define the different categories of savings. Savings are typically placed in categories such as the following:

- *Hard savings* are actual reductions in dollars now being spent, such as reduced budgets, fewer employees, reduction of prices paid on purchasing contracts, etc. Hard savings can be used to lower prices, change bid models, increase profits, or for other purposes where a high degree of confidence in the benefit is required.

- *Soft savings* are projected reductions that should result from the project. For example, savings from less inventory, reduced testing, lower cycle times, improved yields, lower rework rates, and reduced scrap. It is important that savings be integrated into the business systems of the organization. If the institutional framework doesn't change, the savings could eventually be lost. For example, if a Six Sigma project improves a process yield, be sure the MRP system's calculations reflect the new yields.

Lessons Learned: Capture and Replication

It is often possible to apply the lessons learned from a project to other processes, either internally or externally. Most companies have more than one person or organizational unit performing similar or identical tasks. Many also have suppliers and outsourcers that do work similar to that being done internally. By replicating the changes done during a project, the benefits of Six Sigma can be multiplied manifold, often at very minimal cost. Think of it as a form of benchmarking, except that instead of looking for the best-in-class process outside of the company, the Six Sigma project *creates* a best-in-class process and you want to teach the new approach to others within the organization.

Unlike benchmarking, where the seekers of knowledge are already predisposed to change what they are doing, the process owners who might benefit from the knowledge gained during a Six Sigma project may not even be aware that they can benefit from a change. This needs to be considered when planning to share lessons learned. The replication process is a combination of motivating, educating, and selling the target audience on the new approach. Since this requires a different skill set than project work, those who worked the project are often *not* the best ones to sell others on the new approach. They can serve as technical advisors to those who will carry the message to other areas. The Six Sigma function (process excellence) usually takes the lead in developing a system for replication and sharing of lessons learned. Savings from replication are booked as Six Sigma savings.

In addition to the lessons learned about business processes, a great deal will be learned about how to conduct successful projects. In a few years, even a moderately sized Six Sigma effort will complete hundreds or thousands of projects. These project lessons learned should be captured and used to help other project teams. The project lessons learned are usually best expressed in simple narratives by the project Black Belt. The narratives can be indexed by search engines and used by other Black Belts in the organization. The lessons learned database is an extremely valuable asset to the Six Sigma organization.

Appendix

Contents

Worksheet 71. Issues List[*]

Issue #	Description of Issue	Action Needed to Resolve Issue	Responsibility for Leading Task	Target Date	Comment

---

[*] Part of the official project plan.

Issue #	Description of Issue	Action Needed to Resolve Issue	Responsibility for Leading Task	Target Date	Comment

Risk Control Plan

Quality Plan

Cost Control Plan

Schedule Control Plan

Project Change Control Plan

Audit Report

Business Process Change Control Plan

Resource Calendars

Attribute Measurement Error Analysis

Attribute data consist of classifications rather than measurements. Attribute inspection involves determining the classification of an item, e.g., is it "good" or "bad"? The principles of good measurement for attribute inspection are the same as for measurement inspection (Table 18). Thus, conceptually at least, it is possible to evaluate attribute measurement systems in much the same way as we evaluate variables measurement systems. Much less work has been done on evaluating attribute measurement systems. The proposals provided in this book are those I've found to be useful for my employers and clients. The ideas are not part of any standard and you are encouraged to think about them critically before adopting them. I also include an example of MINITAB's attribute gauge R&R analysis.

Table 18. Attribute Measurement Concepts

Measurement Concept	Interpretation for Attribute Data	Suggested Metrics and Comments
Accuracy	Items are correctly categorized.	$$\frac{\text{Number of times correctly classified by all}}{\text{Total number of evaluations by all}}$$ Requires knowledge of the "true" value.
Bias	The proportion of items in a given category is correct.	Overall average proportion in a given category (for all inspectors) minus correct proportion in a given category. Averaged over all categories. Requires knowledge of the "true" value.
Repeatability	When an inspector evaluates the same item multiple times in a short time interval, he or she assigns it to the same category every time.	For a given inspector: $$\frac{\text{Total number of times repeat classifications agree}}{\text{Total number of repeat classifications}}$$ Overall: Average of repeatabilities
Reproducibility	When all inspectors evaluate the same item, they all assign it to the same category.	$$\frac{\text{Total number of times classifications for all concur}}{\text{Total number of classifications}}$$

Measurement Concept	Interpretation for Attribute Data	Suggested Metrics and Comments	
Stability	The variability among attribute R&R studies at different times.	**Metric**	**Stability Measure for Metric**
		Repeatability	Standard deviation of repeatabilities.
		Reproducibility	Standard deviation of reproducibilities.
		Accuracy	Standard deviation of accuracies.
		Bias	Average bias.
"Linearity"	When an inspector evaluates items covering the full set of categories, his or her classifications are consistent across the categories.	Range of inaccuracy and bias across all categories. Requires knowledge of the "true" value. Note: Because there is no natural ordering for nominal data, the concept of linearity doesn't really have a precise analog for attributes data on this scale. However, the suggested metrics will highlight interactions between inspectors and specific categories.	

Operational Definitions

An operational definition is defined as a requirement that includes a means of measurement. "High-quality solder" is a requirement that must be operationalized by a clear definition of what "high-quality solder" means. This might include verbal descriptions, magnification power, photographs, physical comparison specimens, and many more criteria.

Examples of Operational Definitions

1. Ozone Transport Assessment Group (OTAG): Operational Definition of Goal

Goal: To identify reductions and recommend transported ozone and its precursors which, in combination with other measures, will enable attainment and maintenance of the ozone standard in the OTAG region.
Suggested operational definition of the goal:
1) A general modeled reduction in ozone and ozone precursors aloft throughout the OTAG region; and

2) A reduction of ozone and ozone precursors both aloft and at ground level at the boundaries of non-attainment area modeling domains in the OTAG region; and

3) A minimization of increases in peak ground-level ozone concentrations in the OTAG region. (This component of the operational definition is in review.)

2. Wellesley College Child Care Policy Research Partnership: Operational Definition of Unmet Need

1. Standard of comparison to judge the adequacy of neighborhood services: the median availability of services in the larger region (Hampden County).

2. Thus, our definition of unmet need: the difference between the care available in the neighborhood and the median level of care in the surrounding region (stated in terms of child care slots indexed to the age-appropriate child population—"slots-per-tots").

3. Operational Definitions of Acids and Bases

1. An *acid* is any substance that increases the concentration of the H^+ ion when it dissolves in water.

2. A *base* is any substance that increases the concentration of the OH^- ion when it dissolves in water.

4. Operational Definition of "Intelligence"

1. Administer the Stanford-Binet IQ test to a person and score the result. The person's intelligence is the score on the test.

5. Operational Definition of "Dark Blue Carpet"

A carpet will be deemed to be dark blue if

1. Judged by an inspector medically certified as having passed the U.S. Air Force test for color-blindness

2. It matches the PANTONE color card 7462 C when both carpet and card are illuminated by GE "cool white" fluorescent tubes

3. Card and carpet are viewed at a distance between 16 inches and 24 inches.

How to Conduct Attribute Inspection Studies

Some commonly used approaches to attribute inspection analysis are shown in Table 19.

Table 19. Methods of Evaluating Attribute Inspection

True Value	Method of Evaluation	Comments
Known	*Expert Judgment:* An expert looks at the classifications after the operator makes normal classifications and decides which are correct and which are incorrect.	• *Metrics*: Percent correct • Quantifies the accuracy of the classifications. • Simple to evaluate. • Who says the expert is correct? • Care must be taken to include all types of attributes. • Difficult to compare operators since different units are classified by different people. • Acceptable level of performance must be decided upon. Consider cost, impact on customers, etc.
	Round Robin Study: A set of carefully identified objects is chosen to represent the full range of attributes. 1. Each item is evaluated by an expert and its condition recorded. 2. Each item is evaluated by every inspector at least twice.	• *Metrics:* 1. Percent correct by inspector 2. Inspector repeatability 3. Inspector reproducibility 4. Stability 5. Inspector "linearity" • Full range attributes included. • All aspects of measurement error quantified. • People know they're being watched, may affect performance. • Not routine conditions. • Special care must be taken to ensure rigor. • Acceptable level of performance must be decided upon for each type of error. Consider cost, impact on customers, etc.

True Value	Method of Evaluation	Comments

Unknown	*Inspector Concurrence Study:*
	A set of carefully identified objects is chosen to represent the full range of attributes, to the extent possible.
	1. Each item is evaluated by every inspector at least twice.
		• *Metrics:*
		  1. Inspector repeatability
		  2. Inspector reproducibility
		  3. Stability
		  4. Inspector "linearity"
		
		• Like a round robin, except true value isn't known.
		
		• No measures of accuracy or bias are possible. Can only measure agreement between equally qualified people.
		
		• Full range of attributes included.
		
		• People know they're being watched, may affect performance.
		
		• Not routine conditions.
		
		• Special care must be taken to ensure rigor.
		
		• Acceptable level of performance must be decided upon for each type of error. Consider cost, impact on customers, etc.

Example of Attribute Inspection Error Analysis

Two sheets with identical lithographed patterns are to be inspected under carefully controlled conditions by each of the three inspectors. Each sheet has been carefully examined multiple times by journeyman lithographers and they have determined that one of the sheets should be classified as acceptable and the other as unacceptable. The inspectors sit on a stool at a large table where the sheet will be mounted for inspection. The inspector can adjust the height of the stool and the angle of the table. A lighted magnifying glass is mounted to the table with an adjustable arm that lets the inspector move it to any part of the sheet. (See Figure 39.)

Figure 39. Lithography Inspection Station Table, Stool, and Magnifying Glass

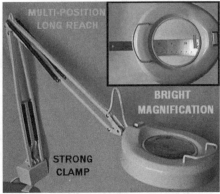

Each inspector checks each sheet once in the morning and again in the afternoon. After each inspection, the inspector classifies the sheet as either acceptable or unacceptable. The entire study is repeated the following week. The results are shown in Table 20.

Table 20. Results of Lithography Attribute Inspection Study

	A	B	C	D	E	F	G	H	I
1	Part	Standard	InspA	InspB	InspC	Date	Time	Reproducible	Accurate
2	1	1	1	1	1	Today	Morning	1	1
3	1	1	0	1	1	Today	Afternoon	0	0
4	2	0	0	0	0	Today	Morning	1	0
5	2	0	0	0	1	Today	Afternoon	0	0
6	1	1	1	1	1	Last Week	Morning	1	1
7	1	1	1	1	0	Last Week	Afternoon	0	0
8	2	0	0	0	1	Last Week	Morning	0	0
9	2	0	0	0	0	Last Week	Afternoon	1	0

In Table 20, the "Part" column identifies which sheet is being inspected and the "Standard" column is the classification for the sheet based on the journeymen's evaluations. A 1 indicates that the sheet is acceptable, a 0 that it is unacceptable. The columns labeled "InspA," "InspB," and "InspC" show the classifications assigned by the three inspectors respectively. The "Reproducible" column is a 1 if *all three* inspectors agree on the classification, whether their classification agrees with the standard or not. The "Accurate" column is a 1 if *all three* inspectors classify the sheet correctly as shown in the "Standard" column.

Individual Inspector Accuracy

Individual inspector accuracy is determined by comparing each inspector's classification with the standard. For example, in cell C2 of Table 20, Inspector A classified the unit as acceptable and the "Standard" column in the same row indicates that the classification is correct. However, in cell C3 the unit is classified as unacceptable when it actually is acceptable. Continuing this evaluation shows that Inspector A made the correct assessment 7 out of 8 times, for an accuracy of 0.875 or 87.5%. The results for all inspectors are given in Table 21.

Table 21. Inspector Accuracies

Inspector	A	B	C
Accuracy	87.5%	100.0%	62.5%

Repeatability and Pairwise Reproducibility

Repeatability is defined in Table 18 as the same inspector getting the same result when evaluating the same item more than once within a short time interval. We see that when InspA evaluated Part 1 in the morning of "Today," she classified it as acceptable (1), but in the afternoon she said it was unacceptable (0). The other three morning/afternoon classifications matched each other. Thus, her repeatability is ¾ or 75%.

Pairwise reproducibility is the comparison of each inspector with every other inspector when checking the same part at the same time on the same day. For example, for Part 1, Morning, Today, InspA's classification matched that of InspB. However, for Part 1, *Afternoon*, Today, InspA's classification was different from that of InspB. There are eight such comparisons for each pair of inspectors. We see that InspA and InspB agreed seven of the eight times, for a pairwise repeatability of $7/8 = 0.88$.

In Table 22, the diagonal values are the repeatability scores and the off-diagonal elements are the pairwise reproducibility scores. The results are shown for "Today," "Last Week," and both combined.

Table 22. Repeatability and Pairwise Reproducibility for Both Days Combined

Overall				Today				Last Week		
	A	B	C		A	B	C		A	B	C
A	0.75	0.88	0.50	A	0.50	0.75	0.50	A	1.00	1.00	0.50
B		1.00	0.50	B		1.00	0.75	B		1.00	0.50
C			0.25	C			0.50	C			0.00

Overall Repeatability, Reproducibility, Accuracy, and Bias

Information is always lost when summary statistics are used, but the data reduction often makes the tradeoff worthwhile. The calculations for the overall statistics are operationally defined as follows:

- *Repeatability* is the average of the repeatability scores for the two days combined, i.e.,

216

$$\frac{0.75 + 1.00 + 0.25}{3} = 0.67$$

- *Reproducibility* is the average of the reproducibility scores for the two days combined (see Table 20), i.e.,

$$\left(\frac{1 + 0 + 1 + 0}{4} + \frac{1 + 0 + 0 + 1}{4} \right) \Big/ 2 = 0.50$$

- *Accuracy* is the average of the accuracy scores for the two days combined (see Table 20), i.e.,

$$\left(\frac{1 + 0 + 0 + 0}{4} + \frac{1 + 0 + 0 + 0}{4} \right) \Big/ 2 = 0.25$$

- *Bias* is the estimated proportion in a category divided by the true proportion in the category. In this example, the true percent defective is 50% (1 part in 2). Of the 24 evaluations, 12 evaluations classified the item as defective. Thus, the bias is $0.5 - 0.5 = 0$.

Overall Stability

Stability is calculated for each of the above metrics separately, as shown in Table 23.

Table 23. Stability Analysis

Stability of ...	Operational Definition of Stability	Stability Result
Repeatability	Standard deviation of the six repeatabilities (0.5, 1, 0.5, 1, 1, 1)	0.41
Reproducibility	Standard deviation of the average repeatabilities. For Table 20, =STDEV(AVERAGE(H2:H5),AVERAGE(H6:H9))	0.00
Accuracy	Standard deviation of the average accuracies. For Table 20, =STDEV(AVERAGE(I2:I5),AVERAGE(I6:I9))	0.00
Bias	Average of bias over the two weeks	0.0

Interpretation of Results

1. The system *overall* appears to be unbiased and accurate. However, the evaluation of individual inspectors indicates that there is room for improvement.

2. The results of the individual accuracy analysis indicate that Inspector C has a problem with accuracy. (See Table 21.)

3. The results of the R&R [pairwise] indicate that Inspector C has a problem with both repeatability and reproducibility. (See Table 22.)

4. The repeatability numbers are not very stable (Table 23). Comparing the diagonal elements for Today with those of Last Week in Table 23, we see that inspectors A

and C tended to get different results for the different weeks. Otherwise, the system appears to be relatively stable.

5. Reproducibility of Inspectors A and B is not perfect. Some benefit might be obtained from looking at reasons for the difference.

6. Since Inspector B's results are more accurate and repeatable, studying her might lead to the discovery of best practices.

MINITAB Attribute Gauge R&R Example

MINITAB includes a built-in capability to analyze attribute measurement systems, known as "attribute gauge R&R." We will repeat the above analysis using MINITAB. MINITAB can't work with the data as shown in Table 20; it must be rearranged. Once the data are in a format acceptable to MINITAB, we enter the Attribute Gauge R&R Study dialog box by choosing Stat > Quality Tools > Attribute Gauge R&R Study. (See Figure 40.) Note the checkbox, "Categories of the attribute data are ordered." Check this box if the data are ordinal and have more than two levels. Ordinal data means, for example, a 1 is in some sense "bigger" or "better" than a 0. For example, we ask raters in a taste test a question like the following: "Rate the flavor as 0 (awful), 1 (OK), or 2 (delicious)." Our data are ordinal ("acceptable" is better than "unacceptable"), but there are only two levels, so we will not check this box.

Figure 40. Attribute Gauge R&R Dialog Box and Data Layout

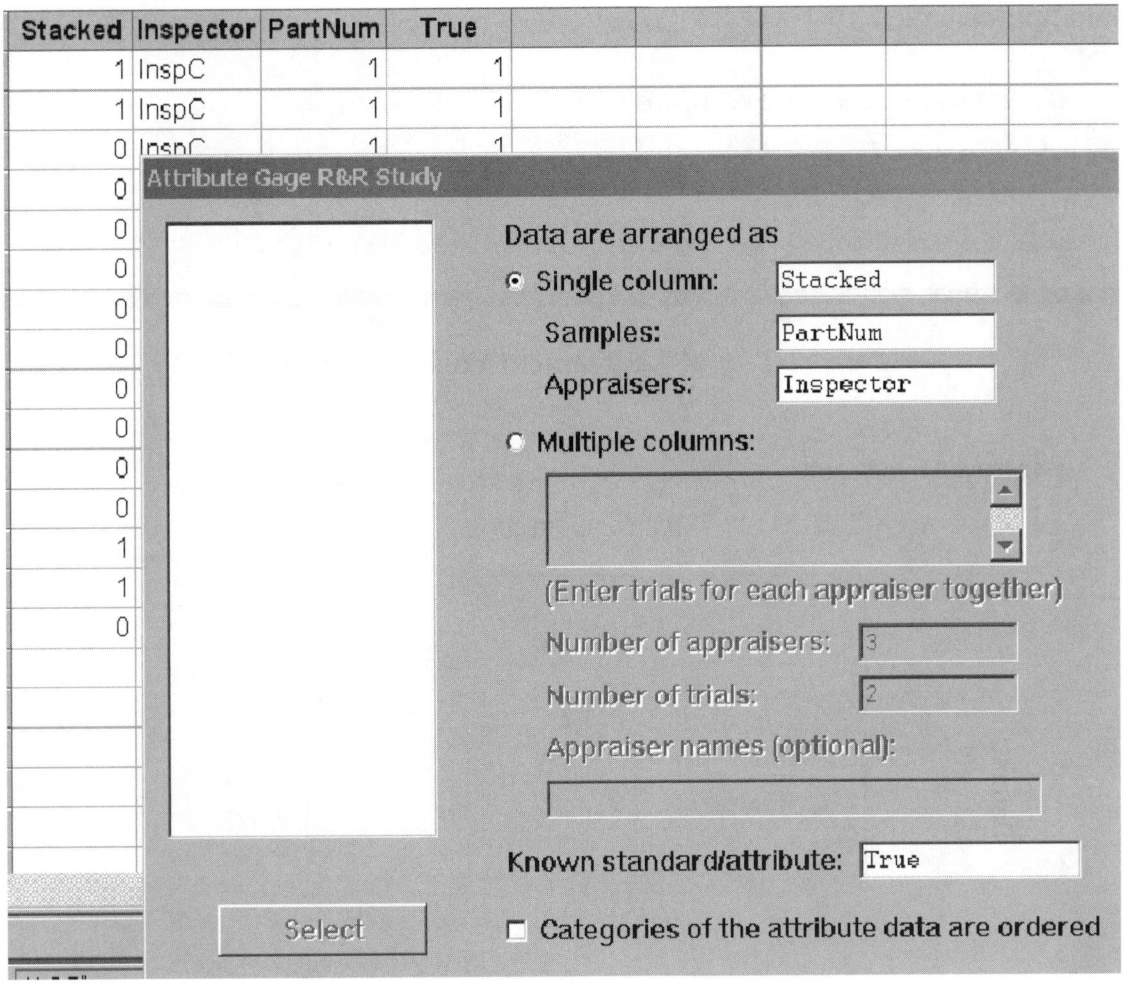

Stacked	Inspector	PartNum	True
1	InspC	1	1
1	InspC	1	1
0	InspC	1	1
0			
0			
0			
0			
0			
0			
0			
0			
0			
1			
1			
0			

Attribute Gage R&R Study

Data are arranged as
- ◉ Single column: `Stacked`
  - Samples: `PartNum`
  - Appraisers: `Inspector`
- ○ Multiple columns:

(Enter trials for each appraiser together)
Number of appraisers: `3`
Number of trials: `2`
Appraiser names (optional):

Known standard/attribute: `True`

Select

☐ Categories of the attribute data are ordered

"Agreement Within Appraiser" Analysis

MINITAB evaluates the repeatability of appraisers by examining how often the appraiser "agrees with himself/herself across trials." It does this by looking at all of the classifications for each part and counting the number of *parts* where *all* classifications agreed. For our example, the appraisers looked at two parts four times each. MINITAB's output, shown in Figure 41, indicates that InspA rated 50% of the parts consistently, InspB 100%, and InspC 0%. The 95% confidence interval on the percentage agreement is also shown. The results are displayed graphically in Figure 42.

Figure 41. MINITAB "Agreement Within Appraiser"

```
Within Appraiser
Assessment Agreement

Appraiser # Inspected # Matched Percent (%)        95.0% CI
InspA             2           1        50.0 (  1.3,  98.7)
InspB             2           2       100.0 ( 22.4, 100.0)
InspC             2           0         0.0 (  0.0,  77.6)

# Matched: Appraiser agrees with himself/herself across trials.
```

Figure 42. Plot of "Agreement Within Appraiser"

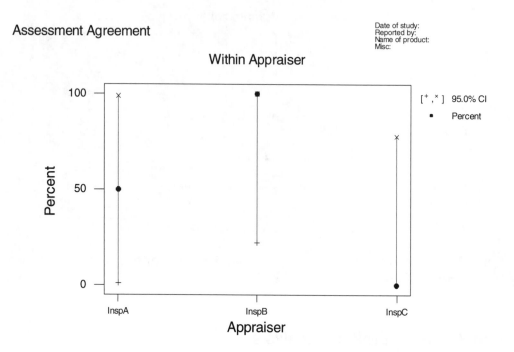

Accuracy Analysis

MINITAB evaluates accuracy by looking at how often all of an appraiser's classify-cations for a given part agree with the standard. Figure 43 shows the results for our example. As before, MINITAB combines the results for both days. The plot of these results is shown in Figure 43.

Figure 43. MINITAB "Agreement of Appraiser and Standard"

```
Each Appraiser vs. Standard
Assessment Agreement

Appraiser # Inspected # Matched Percent (%)        95.0% CI
InspA            2          1        50.0 (  1.3,   98.7)
InspB            2          2       100.0 ( 22.4,  100.0)
InspC            2          0         0.0 (  0.0,   77.6)

# Matched: Appraiser's assessment across trials agrees with standard.
```

Figure 44. Plot of "Agreement of Appraiser and Standard"

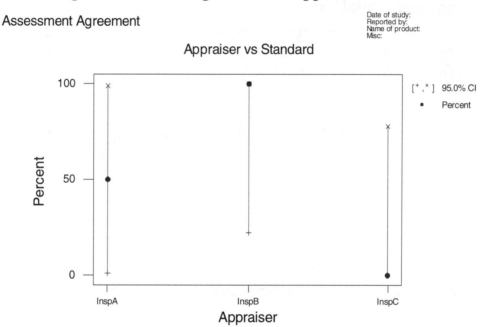

MINITAB also looks at whether or not there is a distinct pattern in the disagreements with the standard. It does this by counting the number of times the appraiser classified an item as a 1 when the standard said it was a 0 (the # 1/0 Percent column), how often the appraiser classified an item as a 0 when it was a 1 (the # 0/1 Percent column), and how often the appraiser's classifications were mixed, i.e., not repeatable (the # Mixed Percent column). The results are shown in Figure 45. The results indicate that there is no consistent bias, defined as consistently putting a unit into the same wrong category. The problem, as shown in the previous analysis, is that appraisers A and C are not repeatable.

221

Figure 45. MINITAB "Appraiser Disagreement"

Assessment Disagreement

Appraiser	# 1/0	Percent (%)	# 0/1	Percent (%)	# Mixed	Percent (%)
InspA	0	0.0	0	0.0	1	50.0
InspB	0	0.0	0	0.0	0	0.0
InspC	0	0.0	0	0.0	2	100.0

```
# 1/0: Assessments across trials = 1 / standard = 0.
# 0/1: Assessments across trials = 0 / standard = 1.
# Mixed: Assessments across trials are not identical.
```

"Between Appraiser" Analysis

Next, MINITAB looks at all of the appraiser assessments for each part and counts how often every appraiser agrees on the classification of the part. The results, shown in Figure 46, indicate that this never happened during our experiment. The 95% confidence interval is also shown.

Figure 46. MINITAB "Agreement Between Appraisers"

Between Appraisers
Assessment Agreement

# Inspected	# Matched	Percent (%)	95.0% CI
2	0	0.0	(0.0, 77.6)

```
# Matched: All appraisers' assessments agree with each other.
```

"All Appraisers vs. Standard" Analysis

Finally, MINITAB looks at all of the appraiser assessments for each part and counts how often every appraiser agrees on the classification of the part and his or her classification agrees with the standard. This can't be any better than the agreement between appraisers shown in Figure 46. Unsurprisingly, the results, shown in Figure 47, indicate that this never happened during our experiment. The 95% confidence interval is also shown.

Figure 47. MINITAB "Assessment vs. Standard Agreement Across All Appraisers"

```
All Appraisers vs. Standard
Assessment Agreement

# Inspected # Matched Percent (%)      95.0% CI
         2         0      0.0 (  0.0,  77.6)

# Matched: All appraisers' assessments agree with standard.
```

Calculating Yields

The rolled throughput yield (RTY) summarizes defects-per-million-opportunities (DPMO) data for a process or product. DPMO is the same as the parts-per-million calculated by MINITAB. RTY is a measure of the *overall* process quality level or, as its name suggests, throughput. For a process, throughput is a measure of what comes out of a process as a function of what goes into it. For a product, throughput is a measure of the quality of the entire product as a function of the quality of its various features. Throughput combines the results of the capability analyses into a measure of overall performance.

To compute the rolled throughput yield for an N-step process (or N-characteristic product), use the following equation:

$$\text{Rolled Throughput Yield} = \left(1 - \frac{DPMO_1}{1,000,000}\right) \times \left(1 - \frac{DPMO_2}{1,000,000}\right) \cdots \left(1 - \frac{DPMO_n}{1,000,000}\right)$$

(Equation 1)

where $DPMO_x$ is defects per million opportunities for step x in the process. For example, consider a four-step process with the following DPMO levels at each step (Table 24).

Table 24. Calculations Used to Find RTY

Process Step	DPMO	Defects per Unit (DPU) =DPMO/1,000,000	1-DPU
1	5,000	0.005000	0.9950
2	15,000	0.015000	0.9850
3	1,000	0.001000	0.9990
4	50	0.000050	0.99995

Rolled Throughput Yield = 0.995 x 0.985 x 0.999 x 0.99995 = 0.979

Figure 48 shows the Excel spreadsheet and formula for this example. The interpretation of the RTY is simple. If you started 1,000 units through this four-step process, you would get only 979 units out the other end. Or, equivalently, to get 1,000 units out of this process, you should start with $\frac{1,000}{0.979} + 1 = 1,022$ units of input. Note that in a series of processes or process steps the RTY is worse than the worst yield of any process or step in the series. It is also worse than the average yield of 0.995. Many a process owner is lulled into complacency by reports showing high average process yields. They are confused by the fact that, despite high average yields, their ratio of end-of-the-line output to starting input is abysmal. Calculating RTY may help open their eyes to what is really going on. The effect of declining RTYs grows exponentially as more process steps are involved.

Figure 48. Excel Spreadsheet for RTY

RTY equation

| B11 | = =D6*D7*D8*D9 |

	A	B	C	D
5	Process Step	DPMO	DPMO/1,0 00,000	1- (DPMO/1,00 0,000)
6	1	5,000	0.005	0.995
7	2	15,000	0.015	0.985
8	3	1,000	0.001	0.999
9	4	50	0.00005	0.99995
10				
11	RTY	0.979046		

The sigma-level equivalent for this four-step process RTY is 3.5. This would be the estimated "process" sigma level. Also see "Normalized Yield and Sigma Level" below.

Using e^{-dpu} to Calculate RTY

If a Poisson distribution is assumed for defects, then the probability of getting exactly x defects on a unit from a process with an average defect rate of μ is $P(x) = \dfrac{\mu^x e^{-\mu}}{x!}$, where $e = 2.71828$. Recall that RTY is the number of units that get through *all* of the processes or process steps with no defects, i.e., $x = 0$. If we let μ = dpu, then the RTY can be calculated as the probability of getting exactly 0 defects on a unit with an average defect rate of dpu, or RTY = e^{-dpu}. However, this approach can be used only when all of the process steps have the same dpu. This is seldom the case. If this approach is used for processes with unequal dpu's, the calculated RTY will underestimate the actual RTY. For the example presented in Table 24, we obtain the following results using this approach:

$$\overline{dpu} = \frac{1}{N}\sum dpu = \frac{1}{4}(0.005 + 0.015 + 0.001 + 0.00005) = 0.005263$$

$$e^{-\overline{dpu}} = e^{-0.005263} = 0.994751$$

225

Note that this is considerably better than the 0.979 RTY calculated above. Since the individual process steps have much different dpu's, the earlier estimate should be used.

Worksheet 70. Rolled Throughput Yields Worksheet

RTY Capability	
RTY Actual	
Project RTY Goal	

Things to consider:
- ❏ How large are the gaps among the actual RTY, the capability RTY, and the project goal RTY?
- ❏ Does actual process performance indicate a need for a breakthrough project?
- ❏ Would we need a breakthrough project if we operated up to capability?
- ❏ Would focusing on a subset of CTx's achieve the project goals at lower cost?

Normalized Yield and Sigma Level

To compute the normalized yield, which is a kind of average, for an N-process or N-product department or organization, use the following equation:

$$\text{Normalized Yield} = \sqrt{\left(1 - \frac{DPMO_1}{1{,}000{,}000}\right) \times \left(1 - \frac{DPMO_2}{1{,}000{,}000}\right) \cdots \left(1 - \frac{DPMO_n}{1{,}000{,}000}\right)}$$

(Equation 2)

For example, consider a four-process organization with the following DPMO levels for each process:

Process	DPMO	DPMO/1,000,000	1-(DPMO/1,000,000)
Billing	5,000	0.005000	0.9950000
Shipping	15,000	0.015000	0.9850000
Manufacturing	1,000	0.001000	0.9990000
Receiving	50	0.000050	0.9999500

$$\text{Normalized Yield} = \sqrt[4]{0.995 \times 0.985 \times 0.999 \times 0.99995} = 0.99472$$

The figure below shows the Excel spreadsheet for this example.

Figure 49. Excel Spreadsheet for Calculating Normalized Yield

	A	B	C	D
1	Process	DPMO	DPMO/1,000,000	1-(DPMO/1,000,000)
2	Billing	5,000	0.005	0.995
3	Shipping	15,000	0.015	0.985
4	Manufacturing	1,000	0.001	0.999
5	Receiving	50	0.000	1.000
6	NY	0.99472		

B6 = =(D2*D3*D4*D5)^0.25 — Normalized yield

The sigma-level equivalent of this four-process organization's normalized yield is 4.1. This would be the estimated "organization" sigma level. Normalized yield should be considered a handy accounting device for measuring overall system quality. Because it is a type of average, it is not necessarily indicative of any particular product or process

227

yield or of how the organization's products will perform in the field. To calculate these, refer to the equation above, at the start of this section.

Solving for a Desired RTY

Assuming every step has an equal yield, it is possible to "backsolve" to find the normalized yield required in order to get a desired RTY for the entire process. (See Equation 6.)

$$Y_n = \sqrt[n]{RTY} = RTY^{\frac{1}{n}}$$ (Equation 6)

where Yn is the yield for an individual process step and N is the total number of steps. If the process yields are not equal, then Yn is the required yield of the worst step in the process. For example, for a 10-step process with a desired RTY of 0.999, the worst acceptable yield for any process step is $Y_n = RTY^{\frac{1}{10}} = (0.999)^{\frac{1}{10}} = 0.9999$.

Finding RTY Using Simulation

Unfortunately, finding the RTY isn't always as straightforward as described above. In the real world, you seldom find a series of process steps all neatly feeding into one another in a nice, linear fashion. Instead, you have different supplier streams, each with different volumes and different yields. There are steps that are sometimes taken and sometimes not. There are test and inspection stations, with imperfect results. There is rework and repair. The list goes on and on. In such cases, it is sometimes possible to trace a particular batch of inputs through the process, monitoring the results after each step. However, it is often exceedingly difficult to control the workflow in the real world. The production and information systems are not designed to provide the kind of tracking needed to get accurate results. The usual outcome of such attempts is questionable data and disappointment.

High-end simulation software offers an alternative. You can model the individual steps, then combine the steps into a process. The software will monitor the results as it "runs the process" as often as necessary to obtain the level of accuracy needed. Figure 50 shows an example. Note that the Properties dialog box is for step 12 in the process ("Right Med?"). The model is programmed to keep track of the errors encountered as a Med Order goes through the process. Statistics are defined to calculate dpu and RTY for the process as a whole. (See the Custom Statistics box in the lower right of Figure 50.) Since the process is non-linear (i.e., it includes feedback loops), it isn't a simple matter to determine which steps would have the greatest impact on RTY. However, the software lets the Black Belt test multiple what-if scenarios to determine this. It can also link to MINITAB or Excel to allow detailed data capture and analysis.

Figure 50. Finding RTY Using Simulation Software[1]

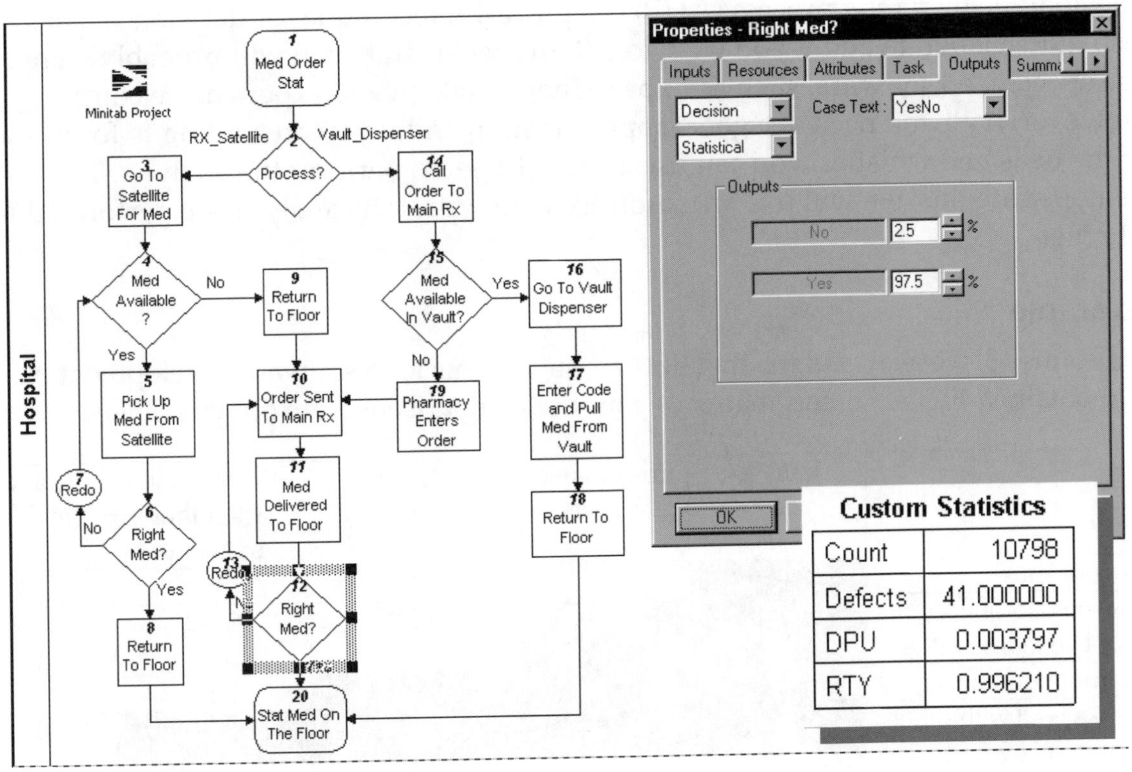

[1] iGrafx Process for Six Sigma, Corel Corporation.

Analytic Hierarchy Process (AHP) Using MS Excel

The analytic hierarchy process (AHP) is a powerful technique for decision-making. It is also quite elaborate and if you wish to obtain exact results you will probably want to use specialized software, such as Expert Choice 2000 (www.expertchoice.com). However, if all you need is a good approximation and if you are willing to forgo some of the bells and whistles, you can use a spreadsheet to perform the analysis. To demonstrate this, we will use Microsoft Excel to repeat the analysis we performed in Chapter 3.

Example

In Chapter 3, we analyzed the high-level requirements for a software development process and obtained Figure 36, this matrix of pairwise comparisons from our customers.

	Easy to learn	Easy to use quickly	Internet connectivity	Works well with other software	Easy to maintain
Easy to learn		4	1	3	1
Easy to use quickly after I've learned it			0.20	0.33	0.25
Internet connectivity				3	3
Works well with other software I own					0.33
Easy to maintain	Incon: 0.05				

The meaning of the numbers is described in Chapter 3. The Excel equivalent of this matrix is:

		B	C	D	E	F
A						
1	Attribute	A	B	C	D	E
2	A-Easy to learn	0.00	4.00	1.00	3.00	1.00
3	B-Easy to use	0.25	0.00	0.20	0.33	0.25
4	C-Connectivity	1.00	5.00	0.00	3.00	3.00
5	D-Compatible	0.33	3.00	0.33	0.00	0.33
6	E-Easy to maintain	1.00	4.00	0.33	3.00	0.00

Note that some numbers in the original matrix have become reciprocals, e.g., the 5.0 in row 3, column 4 is now 0.20, or 1/5. These were negative numbers in the original matrix. All of the numbers in rows 3 and 5 of the original matrix are negative and are shown as reciprocals in the Excel matrix. The numbers on the diagonal are zeros; the comparison of an attribute with itself has no meaning. Finally, the numbers below the diagonals are the reciprocals of the corresponding comparison above the diagonal; e.g., cell C2 has a 4.00, indicating that attribute A is preferred over attribute B, so cell B3 must contain ¼ = 0.25 to show that preference.

To calculate the weight for each item, we must obtain the grand total for the entire matrix and then divide the row totals by the grand total. This procedure, called *normalizing*, is shown below:

		B	C	D	E	F
A						
1	Attribute	A	B	C	D	E	Total	Weight
2	A-Easy to learn	0.00	4.00	1.00	3.00	1.00	9.00	**26.2%**
3	B-Easy to use	0.25	0.00	0.20	0.33	0.25	1.03	**3.0%**
4	C-Connectivity	1.00	5.00	0.00	3.00	3.00	12.00	**34.9%**
5	D-Compatible	0.33	3.00	0.33	0.00	0.33	4.00	**11.6%**
6	E-Easy to maintain	1.00	4.00	0.33	3.00	0.00	8.33	**24.2%**
7	**Grand Total**						**34.37**	

These results are shown in the figure below.

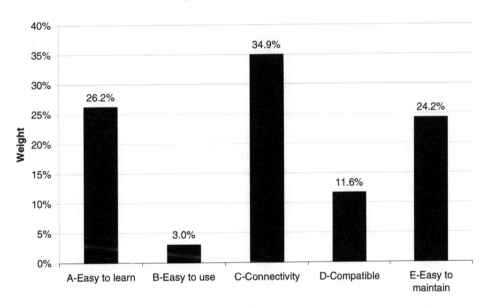

Category Importance Weights

Compare these weights with those obtained by the exact analysis using Expert Choice 2000.

Category	Exact Weight	Spreadsheet Weight
Easy to learn	26.4%	26.2%
Easy to use quickly after I've learned it	5.4%	3.0%
Internet connectivity	35.8%	34.9%
Works well with other software I own	10.5%	11.6%
Easy to maintain	21.8%	24.2%

Additional Resources on Six Sigma Project Management

Books

Duncan, William R. (1996). *A Guide to the Project Management Body of Knowledge.* Newtown Square, PA: Project Management Institute.

Goldratt, Eliyahu M. (1990). *The Haystack Syndrome: Sifting Information Out of the Data Ocean.* Great Barrington, MA: North River Press.

Hillier, Frederick S., and Gerald J. Lieberman. (1980). *Introduction to Operations Research,* 3rd Ed. San Francisco, CA: Holden-Day, Inc.

Pyzdek, Thomas. (2000). *The Six Sigma Handbook.* New York: McGraw-Hill.

Project Management Software

Microsoft Project™ is a general purpose project management software package. *Project* implements the traditional project management model. There is a learning curve required to master the software and its use is generally limited to Black Belts and Master Black Belts. Newer versions of the software allow teams to collaborate over the Internet or corporate intranets. Enterprise project management capabilities, such as sharing of resources across multiple projects, are also available.

ProChain® Project Scheduling is a scheduling and decision support tool that aids the understanding, implementation, and institutionalizing of the Critical Chain improvement concepts presented in Eliyahu Goldratt's book about project management and scheduling, *Critical Chain* (Great Barrington, MA: North River Press, 1997). ProChain provides capabilities to analyze projects, create critical chain schedules, and track those schedules to ensure on-time or early completion. www.prochain.com.

Notes

Notes

Notes

Notes

Notes

Notes

Notes

Notes

Notes

Notes

Notes

Notes